Penguin Health

Living with Allergies

After qualifying in medicine from Cambridge University,
Dr John McKenzie held training posts at several different
London teaching hospitals and developed interests in
allergy and respiratory medicine. He is now a specialist in
diseases of the chest at a leading London teaching hospital.

DR JOHN McKENZIE

LIVING WITH ALLERGIES

PENGUIN BOOKS

Penguin Books Ltd, 27 Wrights Lane, London w8 5tz (Publishing and Editorial)
and Harmondsworth, Middlesex, England (Distribution and Warehouse)
Viking Penguin Inc., 40 West 23rd Street, New York, New York 10010, USA
Penguin Books Australia Ltd, Ringwood, Victoria, Australia
Penguin Books Canada Ltd, 2801 John Street, Markham, Ontario, Canada l3r 1b4
Penguin Books (NZ) Ltd, 182–190 Wairau Road, Auckland 10, New Zealand

First published 1987

Made and printed in Great Britain by
Richard Clay Ltd, Bungay, Suffolk

Filmset in Monophoto Sabon

To Liz

CONTENTS

8 · Contents

ACKNOWLEDGEMENTS

I am greatly indebted to many friends and expert colleagues who have taken an interest in this book and have made many corrections and suggestions to the various parts of the text. Whatever is good about it is largely due to them. My particular thanks are due to Miriam Seed, who typed and re-typed the manuscript with enormous speed and efficiency – and never complained.

PREFACE

Allergies are important because they are common and often disabling. About one in five of us will have an allergy at some stage during our lives. It may be mild and last for a short time so that we suffer little, or it may be severe and give us unpleasant symptoms for years. Allergies can be confusing, as they take many shapes and forms.

This book aims to give a short, practical guide to allergies and to help you understand more about them. First it describes the workings of the basic allergic reaction, what allergies are, how we get them, and how so many different symptoms can be due to allergy. The details of the many allergies are then given in turn, together with an explanation of how they can be diagnosed and treated by doctors. What you can do for yourself or your child if either of you has an allergy is also explored. We then take a look at what alternative medicine has to offer the allergy sufferer.

This book contains information from many different sources. It is not a complete account – much more could be said – but it is hoped that the basics are covered. I have emphasized areas of controversy or ignorance in the hope of allaying some of the fears and anxieties that allergy sufferers have. We just do not have all the answers to the allergy problem.

Finally, this is *not* a self-help book. It is just a simple guide to the facts for your information and better understanding. Hopefully it will remove some of the mystique and confusion that surrounds allergy. If you develop symptoms that you think are allergic, you should see your own doctor for diagnosis and treatment. This is by far the best course of action and the one most likely to bring about a solution. You may be convinced you have an allergy, but you may be wrong. Your symptoms may be due to something else.

PART ONE

Chapter One

Introduction

What is allergy?

The first part of this book deals with some basic issues which are very important to understanding what allergy is all about. It deals with what an allergic reaction is and how it works in the body to produce symptoms. This is a worthwhile study, as, when we come to describe each allergy in detail together with symptoms and treatment, an overall picture will be much more easily grasped.

So, to start at the beginning: what is allergy? An allergy is an altered reactivity in a person to a particular substance in the environment. Strawberries, pollen grains, jewellery and house dust are basically innocuous items which pass unnoticed by the majority, yet in the allergic person they may provoke severe symptoms. So the allergic person has this abnormal capacity to react to very ordinary and commonly encountered substances. Doctors and scientists limit the word allergy to include only altered states of reactivity due to immune reactions in the body. (Immune reactions are explained in Chapter 2.) As most allergic diseases, as they are understood in scientific terms at the moment, are due to such immune reactions, we will adopt the same limitation of usage in this book. There is often misunderstanding about exactly what allergy is, and our definition immediately raises two problems. The first is semantic, when 'allergy' is used figuratively. If I say that I am allergic to cricket, or to the Sunday papers, I simply mean that I dislike them, and not that I am having an immune reaction to them. Secondly, not everything that makes us feel ill or gives us symptoms does so because of an immune reaction. This is particularly true of food. Many items in the diet can give us various unpleasant symptoms, without these being due to an allergy in the strict sense. Food intolerance and other food reactions are probably not due to food allergy. The same applies to 'total body allergy' and 'allergy to the twentieth century'. Whatever these conditions might be, they are not strictly due to allergic reactions.

The main point is that there are other possible ways besides allergic reactions in which various things in our environment can harm us. If someone has an allergy it is because he is making an immune response to a totally harmless substance. Usually immune responses protect us, but allergic reactions do not. Not only are they useless, they actually cause disease.

Why is allergy important?

Allergies are common. At least 20 per cent of the population will suffer from allergic symptoms at some time in their lives. Allergies involve vast numbers of people. It has been estimated, for example, that there are 35 million allergy sufferers in the USA. Allergy is a global problem: no country or state is exempt. The symptoms that allergy sufferers have may seem rather trivial compared with other sorts of disease, but they can be enormously disabling and incapacitating. Everyone is familiar with the example of the anxious teenager, coming up to important school exams in the summer, who then gets severe hayfever which, if not successfully treated, makes exam-taking virtually impossible.

Having intolerable constant itching of the eyes, nose and throat, continuous sneezing, watering of the eyes so that you can scarcely see, and a running blocked nose which interferes with breathing is no trivial matter. Such symptoms make sleeping impossible, let alone working for exams, and make the severe hayfever case incapable of doing anything. Such symptoms are full-time misery. Yet hayfever is often regarded as the mildest form of allergy. At least hayfever only lasts as long as the pollen season. Other allergic complaints can produce symptoms all the year round. Allergic disorders are fortunately only very rarely fatal (for example, the massive allergic reaction which may follow a bee-sting), but they can be extremely chronic and give disabling symptoms that last for years. Some chronic allergies are serious illnesses in their own right apart from the unpleasant symptoms, and need complicated treatment. For example, a proportion of asthma cases are due to allergy. Asthma is a potential killer, and can interfere greatly with normal everyday life. Now the vast majority of asthmatics can enjoy virtually symptom-free lives, thanks to modern treatment. It is obvious that, because of the disability and disruption allergy causes, it has repercussions within the family and society generally. Time lost from school and work has important economic and social consequences, and these are made worse if allergies develop to substances present at the work place. Luckily many allergies are now well understood and treatment is often effective in minimizing the damage.

Allergies are also important for the anxiety and stress they cause, both to the allergy sufferer and to the rest of the family. This is particularly true for parents of allergic children. Also, stress, anxiety and tension can make allergic symptoms worse, or even bring attacks on. It is easy for allergic children and the family to get into a vicious circle of increasing anxiety, increasing family discord, and increasingly bad symptoms. The general anxiety that surrounds allergy is made worse if there are misconceptions and misunderstandings about what it is, the way it is likely to behave and how it will respond to treatment. Surprisingly, many allergic patients have wrong beliefs about their problems despite having had allergies for years. If misunderstandings can be corrected, the fear and panic that so often goes with an allergy can be greatly reduced.

The range of allergic disorders

Allergies can lead to a wide range of symptoms, reflecting the wide spectrum of allergic disorder. Although allergies are so varied, they are all due by and large to a single underlying mechanism which we will outline in the next two chapters. Many cases of allergy, fortunately, have only mild symptoms that do not interfere too greatly with normal life, whereas an unlucky minority are severely affected. Similarly, allergies may be transient and last only a few months, or may persist for years without respite. There is an enormous range of substances to which allergy can develop. We come across many of these in our daily environment. These are substances from animals, plants, fungi, manufactured goods and chemicals. In the increasingly complex world in which we live, new substances are constantly appearing to which we may become allergic both in the home and at work. For example, new synthetic substances are increasingly used in food processing, and the variety of environments in which we have to work and live is greater than ever before.

Where allergies differ from other diseases

Allergic diseases differ in some quite striking ways from other types of disease. Firstly they are very common. But so are heart attacks and cancer, you may say. There is an important difference though, and that is that heart attacks, cancer, arthritis and bronchitis on the whole attack later in life and they may very often have a fatal outcome. Allergies usually start early in life and can run on from the cradle to the grave. In fact, the majority of allergy sufferers will have symptoms well before their tenth birthday. This duration of symptoms makes allergies different from the common infections, for example, pneumonia, gastroenteritis or a sore throat, which usually clear up in a week or so with treatment. Our understanding of allergy is now quite good, yet treatment is not always entirely satisfactory. Although symptoms can usually be improved, they may still be there to cause disability and misery. Added to the list of well-known allergies like hayfever there is a large collection of conditions that are not yet understood and that may have an allergic component. These 'possible allergies' may include migraine, some sorts of digestive trouble, some types of arthritis, and behaviour disturbance in children. Add to all this the misconceptions that people can have about allergy, and it is hardly surprising that allergy generally causes so much trouble all round.

The medical profession

It is sometimes said that allergy sufferers often have difficulty in getting help, advice, and satisfactory treatment for their condition. Why is this? In fact, the majority of patients with allergies are probably correctly diagnosed and treated, yet one still hears of allergy sufferers receiving unsympathetic treatment from their doctors, who may adopt a sceptical attitude. There are several reasons why this is so. Allergy generally falls into one of two classes. The first is when diagnosis and treatment is obvious, quick and effective. If I eat shellfish and come out in a massive attack of itchy red lumps within a few minutes, common sense rules. I do not have to be told by a doctor that I must not have shellfish again. If I get terrible itching and watering of the nose and eyes when the pollen count is very high, then obviously I have hayfever and there are remedies which will be effective in most cases. The second class of allergy is much more difficult. The time relation with the substance that triggered off the allergic attack may not be clear-cut, the symptoms may be chronic and vague and easily confused with a host of other medical conditions. Even if the condition is finally diagnosed as being allergic in origin, treatment may be difficult or unsuccessful. It is this second class of allergy that tries the patience of doctor and patient alike, and where the patient-doctor relationship may not run so smoothly. The patient becomes frustrated by persistent troublesome symptoms for which there seems to be no adequate explanation and for which treatment fails. The doctor also becomes frustrated by the chronic symptoms that do not clear up with treatment. The extremely irritating nature of chronic allergic symptoms means that time and patience may be required by both doctor and patient to sort an allergy out properly.

Doctors, like any other group of people, have many different viewpoints and opinions. Some are sympathetic and some have a special interest in allergic diseases. Others are not so interested, and may feel that half an hour spent with someone who has just had a heart attack is more worthwhile than half an hour spent with an allergy patient who has a multitude of vague symptoms that persist despite treatment. Family practitioners are often very busy, and allergy takes time. Allergies are very inconvenient to have but are not usually a major hazard to health. Often the doctor does not have time to explain this fully. Other doctors may regard the allergy sufferer as being neurotic and the symptoms as being 'all in the mind'. Of course, some patients with vague chronic symptoms ascribed to allergy are suffering from a neurotic or other mental disturbance – but others may have underlying non-allergic more serious disease. It is up to the skilled physician to sort this out. Certainly other diseases can produce symptoms that can be confused with allergy. If you have persistent troublesome symptoms, go to the doctor and let him decide.

But there may be further reasons to explain the doctor's lack of sympathy. There are two themes running through modern medicine that are closely linked and which may work to reduce serious interest in allergy generally. Modern medicine relies heavily on the following model for the way it goes about business. The model is that symptoms stem from an underlying pathological process in the body. The symptoms guide the doctor to do tests which reveal this process and make a diagnosis. Once this is done, the doctor's aim is to attack, treat or try to reverse the disease process and then the symptoms will go away. Both doctor and patient are satisfied. The doctor can also apply scientific methods to his work, and measure the disease process before and after treatment. For example, many sophisticated measurements can now be made on the heart, allowing extremely precise diagnosis. This is the basis of the clinical controlled therapeutic trial, which is the gold standard used in modern medicine to judge the effectiveness of a new treatment. Allergy does not always fit comfortably into this mould, and this may be a major stumbling block. Allergy is rich in symptoms but poor in measurable underlying disease processes. True, there are levels of antibody in the blood that can be measured, and skin tests can be done, but that is about all and, anyway, these are often poorly related to the allergy symptoms. To make matters worse, in some conditions where allergy may play a part, antibody and other tests are repeatedly negative, so there is nothing to measure. To compound the felony, if we have to rely on symptoms, they are notoriously difficult to measure because they are so subjective. Any trial of a new anti-allergy treatment can be criticized and is likely to founder because it falls short of the requirements of scientific precision needed by doctors and medical scientists to accept the results. Even if symptoms could be measured accurately, they are so variable in allergy that studies would still be difficult.

The second theme is modern medicine's reliance on modern technology. The 'high-tech' approach has brought untold benefits to sufferers of serious potentially fatal diseases – heart surgery for coronary artery disease, kidney transplants for renal failure and the revolution in treatment for leukaemia and cancers, to name but a few examples. The back-wash of all this activity has been a swing away from 'symptom-based' medicine and has left allergy rather the Cinderella in the overall view of things. But exciting developments in immunology and molecular biology research may very soon bring major benefits to allergy victims too.

Controversies in allergy

There is no subject quite like allergy to trigger a lot of heated debate. It is a subject on which doctors, health care workers and patients alike can hold very firm and often quite extreme views. Some of the reasons for this we have touched on already. A wide spectrum of views on allergy is seen within the medical and allied professions. At one end of this spectrum is the view that allergy is really 'all in the mind'. The other extreme is the view held by the recently founded discipline of clinical ecology, which holds that a bewildering array of diseases and disability that no one previously thought had anything to do with allergy are, in fact, all allergic after all. Apart from these extreme views, there are the difficult questions as to whether the 'possible allergies' we mentioned earlier really do have an allergic basis. It is possible that some of these conditions are triggered by allergic reactions to hitherto unidentified things in the environment.

None of this is very helpful to the individual allergy sufferer. How do you know if a symptom you have is allergic? Who will help you find out? When should you discuss it with the doctor? The aim of this book is to give practical common sense advice to the allergy sufferer, despite the often incomplete and uncertain nature of the knowledge that we have about allergy. Everyone is scared of being ill and is anxious to do anything they can themselves to return to health. We will try and emphasize what you can do for yourself to minimize your symptoms.

The medical services for allergy sufferers

Some feel that allergic disease is adequately catered for by the existing services, but others think that far more should be done. In the United Kingdom, most allergy is treated by family practitioners, chest physicians, dermatologists or gastro-enterologists, depending on the organ affected and the severity of the symptoms. In some countries things are different. In the USA, for example, there is a recognized speciality in allergy, so that much allergy is treated by allergy specialists. Many of these allergy specialists are also physicians in internal medicine or paediatricians who have developed a special interest. The difference in services provided in the UK and the USA reflects to an extent in noticeable differences in approach to diagnosis and treatment. In the USA there is far greater emphasis on doing quite complex laboratory tests on allergy patients and using courses of hyposensitization injections in treatment, whereas in the UK the tendency is to use medicines more than injections and to do fewer tests. A further factor accounting for differences in practice is of course that health care resources in the UK are less than in the USA, and this also influences medical practice.

Doctors in the UK have on the whole resisted attempts to establish allergy as a separate medical speciality, and whether this is a good or a bad thing remains open for debate.

Food allergy

The ancient Greeks were probably the first on record to be interested in the relation between food and health. Hippocrates stressed the importance of diet to good health. Pythagoras banned the eating of beans, and Plato advocated a plain diet to ensure a long life. Over the past twenty years, the medical profession has been accused of being very slow to recognize the importance of the effect of diet on health. Now things are changing as the evidence comes in. Links between high animal fat, high carbohydrate, low residue diets and an increased incidence of heart disease, diabetes, bowel disease and possibly some types of cancer are becoming clear. Many people in the Western world are now taking part in the silent revolution and are drastically changing their diets by reducing fat and carbohydrate and increasing the amount of fibre they eat.

The whole subject of food allergy and intolerance has become a focus of attention over the last decade for patients, doctors and alternative practitioners alike. It remains a very difficult and fascinating area, and raises many problems that we will have to examine closely later in this book. It is not very surprising that some of us have adverse reactions to certain foods, in view of the vast range of different items in our diets. Food can contain poisonous materials, or substances that have direct effects that produce symptoms in the digestive system or other organs. For example, some people develop palpitation following too much coffee, and others develop migraine after eating chocolate. These reactions are probably not allergic in the sense we mentioned earlier.

Food allergy can be difficult to prove, whereas allergy to pollen or house dust is usually easy. This is why many doctors remain sceptical. Food allergy has been blamed for a vast collection of diseases, from arthritis to schizophrenia. There are some who believe that food allergy and intolerance is involved in some conditions like the irritable bowel syndrome, migraine, asthma, rhinitis, eczema and urticaria. Yet if someone came up with a diet that cured allergy, high blood pressure, obesity, depression, stomach ulcers, colitis, and asthma, it would be an immediate success and few would oppose it.

Obviously life is more complicated than some advocates of diet as a cure-all would suggest. However, even if a sceptical view is taken, it is at least possible that certain diseases, if not caused by constituents of our diet, may be aggravated by them and some of these might work through allergic mechanisms as well as through direct effects due to food intolerance. The case remains open, and it has yet to be proven that those vague symptoms that are so difficult to pin down to a definite cause are genuinely due to food allergy. Food allergy is attracting increasing attention, yet the difficulty of doing studies on patients which will give clear-cut helpful answers are great. Certainly the vague but disabling symptoms that plague all of us, like headache, irritability, fatigue, insomnia, depression and feeling off colour, deserve further investigation. The problem is how?

A historical note

As usual, the Greeks were there first. Hippocrates described asthma in the fifth century BC. More recently, in 1819, John Bostock described hayfever in London, and in 1872 Wyman showed that pollen was the cause. It remains the commonest and probably best understood of all allergies. In 1902, Richet and Portier in Paris described the massive and often fatal allergic reaction called anaphylaxis (which we will discuss later). The word 'allergy' was first used by Clemens von Pirquet in 1906 to describe the 'altered capacity to react', that is, the abnormal reactivity some people have to common substances. In 1911, Noon injected pollen extracts into hayfever victims in an attempt to immunize them against it. In 1921, Prausnitz and Kustner, two German scientists, did an important experiment to show that allergy was due to something in the allergic patient's blood serum. This was identified in 1967 by a husband and wife team, the doctors Ishizaka, as being a special sort of antibody called Immunoglobulin-E (IgE). In the same year Voorhorst identified the house dust mite (a tiny insect that lives in bedding) as an important cause of allergy.

Since 1967 there have been enormous developments in both science and medicine, and as some knowledge of how the immune system works is vital to understanding allergy, the next chapter gives a brief and hopefully painless guide through the basics of the immune system.

Chapter Two

The Immune System.
How It Works and What It Is For

This chapter explains how the immune system works in protecting the body from disease. This may seem rather remote from our main subject, but a grounding in the basics of immunology will be very useful in allowing a sound understanding of allergic diseases. The reason for this is that all allergic reactions are, in fact, immunological reactions, but immunological reactions with a difference. Instead of protecting us from disease, as many immune reactions do, the allergic reaction actually creates disease. Also, of all the biological sciences, immunology is the one that has distinguished itself with enormous progress over the last quarter of a century, so that our understanding of the way it works, although far from complete, is rapidly becoming very much more clear. This new knowledge should eventually lead to improved treatments and possibly even cures for allergic diseases. Those readers who cannot face a little science so early on, or are already familiar with the basics of immunology, should skip this chapter and return to it later on if they find it necessary.

What is the purpose of the immune system?

The immune system protects us from the unfriendly environment that we all have to live in. We have to share our environment with a myriad of bacteria, viruses, fungi, parasites, particles from animals, chemicals, and poisonous substances. These 'germs' are all present in the air we breathe, the food we eat, and the objects in contact with our skin. We come across them all in the normal course of everyday life and, also, far more after minor injuries. Minor injuries, particularly to the skin, are for most of us an almost daily occurrence (look at the number of bumps, bruises, scratches, grazes and cuts you collect each week).

Our bodies actually provide highly desirable feeding grounds for these germs, so the main purpose of the immune system is to protect us from invasion and destruction by them. The immune system is therefore our internal security system. It 'polices' all our tissues and defends our natural barriers, be they the skin, the digestive system, the lungs, or any contact we have with the outside world.

How does the immune system cope with this daunting task so effectively?

The key feature of the immune system is its ability to spot outsiders, that is, foreign substances. In other words, the immune system can identify all the internal component parts of the body and leave them alone, while at the same time it can spot and tackle an intruder. So any virus or bacteria that enters the body will trigger the immune system into action, leading to a reaction which has a good chance of destroying the intruder. The immune system is therefore crucial to our health. Damage to it results in an increased risk of infection, and, if the system fails altogether, death from overwhelming infection is inevitable without intensive treatment.

The hallmark of the immune response is that it is tailor-made for the particular bacteria or virus causing the infection, a bit like a key exactly fitting a lock. If we catch measles, the immune response deals specifically with the measles. As well as this kind of precise immune protection against 'outsiders', we also have several other important defences (though not strictly immunological) which give some general protection against all potential infectious agents. These operate closely with the immune system, and as they are so important we will look at them first.

General forms of protection from the environment

1. NATURAL BARRIERS

First we have natural barriers that separate us from the outside world. Our skin is a good example, and is usually only breached by bacteria and dirt after an injury, although certain things can seep through it and cause problems as we shall see later. Our connection with the environment is far more intimate when we come to the lung and the digestive system. Here the barrier cannot be thick and impermeable, because for example the lung has to absorb oxygen from the air into the bloodstream. This has to take place across a very thin moist barrier or membrane which is far more vulnerable to attack, and is easily breached. It has been estimated that the total surface area of this membrane inside the lungs is equivalent to the surface area of two tennis courts. To make matters worse, we breathe in about 10,000 to 20,000 litres of air per day. The air we breathe is loaded with bacteria, dust, pollen grains, fungal spores, viruses, smoke, fumes, and so on. As we breathe such a large volume of air full of potential hazards and expose to it such a large surface area of delicate membrane, how does the lung protect itself?

The answer is that from the nose right down to the air sacs in the lung there are systems for filtering and clearing the air of all this rubbish. The large particles get stuck in the nose and mouth and go no further. Particles that are small enough to get into the lung and become deposited there are usually cleared in one of three ways. First, they may be taken up by white blood cells and digested. Second, they may land on the moist lining of the air sacs and bronchial tubes of the lung. This lining is covered in minute hairs called cilia which waft to and fro rather like a field of wheat in the wind (Fig. 1). The effect of this is to shift watery secretions (and any particles that are trapped in them) from the air sacs up through the bronchial tubes to the mouth and out of the body.

And finally there is coughing. When we cough, an explosive jet of air forces the mucus containing the particles up and out into the mouth.

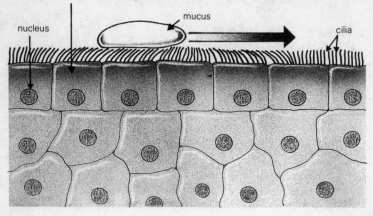

Fig. 1. Clearance of mucus by cilia on the lining of the bronchial tubes.

The digestive system is just as vulnerable. Here, food has to be absorbed across a thin membrane which again presents an opportunity for the germs often found in food to enter our bodies. The acidity of the stomach secretions kills and fortunately provides a great deal of protection against many germs. When we look at allergy and the things to which we can become allergic, it is not surprising that the nose and lung, the digestive system and the skin form the main trouble spots.

2. SECRETIONS

The second kind of general protection is through secretions. Saliva, tears, sweat, bronchial mucus, nasal secretions and gastric juice all contain powerful substances that in various ways discourage and kill germs. They also help wash down and clear the surfaces they are secreted from.

3. WHITE BLOOD CELLS

The third important general protection is brought about by white blood cells. These cells, which are made in the bone marrow, are the scavenger cells of the body. They are released by the marrow

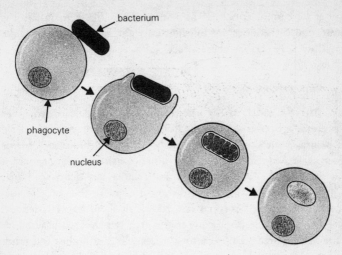

Fig. 2. A white blood cell eating a particle.

into the blood stream, from where they enter all the tissues of the body and patrol them, ingesting and digesting any foreign particles that they encounter. The process involved is highly complex but is obviously a most important and effective way of removing foreign material (Fig. 2). Basically the white cell wraps itself around the germ or particle and eats it. This eating process is enormously increased if the germ is coated in antibody, as we shall see in a moment.

How important are these general defences?

The short answer is that they are vital. If one or more of our defence systems breaks down, the result is the same, namely, severe infection. When the skin is badly damaged after, say, burns, overwhelming infection commonly follows and may kill. If there is a defect in our secretions (as happens in cystic fibrosis) chronic repeated infection is the outcome. If there is an absence of white blood cells for some reason, potentially fatal infections are inevitable. Even if we are deprived of our cough-reflex which protects our airway, we are prone to chest infections and pneumonia. An example of this is the alcoholic who drinks until he is unconscious, so that he cannot cough. If he vomits, he is likely to inhale the vomit, and if this does not kill him outright, he will at least wake up with a very serious chest infection.

Our response to injury

After an injury, all these general defence systems join together to preserve a barrier against the outside world. For example, if we cut or graze our skin it bleeds briefly but then a blood clot forms which seals the breach. Within the blood clot there is an outpouring of white blood cells which engulf and remove any debris and dirt. If dirt or germs causing infection are present in the cut, the surrounding tissue will become red, tense, swollen, hot and tender. This acute inflammation is due to the greatly increased blood flow in the injured area enabling white blood cells, antibodies and other factors to get to the injury site, combat the infection, and organize the healing process.

All these defence systems deal with the vast majority of confrontations with harmful agents. However, even when all is working well, we can still get viral (e.g. colds, flu, mumps and measles) and bacterial (e.g. pneumonia, whooping cough, tuberculosis) infections, from organisms that are able to bypass these systems. It is here that the precise and specific immune system intervenes and helps.

The immune system and its importance

We only get some infectious diseases once. Second attacks of measles, mumps or chicken pox are almost unheard of. Why is this? It is because the first attack protects us against getting a second attack. During the first attack, antibody is produced by the immune system. Antibodies are substances that can recognize and kill the germs that cause infectious diseases and they are very important in recovery from the infection. The antibody produced serves a second function as well. It stays in the body so that if the same germ is encountered again, the antibody neutralizes it before it can cause an infection. Thus a second attack of the infectious disease is prevented. In fact a second encounter with the organism actually boosts the immune system so that even more antibody is produced, increasing protection still further. It is easy to see how vital it is to have a healthy immune system.

The main features of the immune system

We can sum up, then, the main ways in which the immune system works. First, through antibodies that neutralize germs. Second, the antibodies are tailor-made and are produced directly against a germ in a precise way. Third, the immune system remembers each particular germ so that next time it is encountered there is no infection.

How does the immune response work?

First of all we must say what an antigen is. An antigen is a molecule that stimulates an immune response, that is, it leads for example, to the production of antibody.

Bacteria, viruses and other germs have many antigens on their surfaces, all of which are unique (like a code name or signature tune) to those organisms. During the course of an infection by a germ, its antigens are recognized by special white blood cells called lymphocytes, which are made in the bone marrow like the white blood cells which scavenge and eat particles. But lymphocytes do not scavenge and digest. Their role is to recognize these antigens, and to respond by dividing and forming many activated daughter cells.

As there are millions of different antigens, so there are millions of different lymphocytes to match exactly each particular antigen like a key fitting a lock (Fig. 3). There are two main types of lymphocyte: B lymphocytes and T lymphocytes. B lymphocytes when they recognize an antigen rapidly divide, and the activated daughter cells develop into cells that make enormous amounts of antibody which is released into the circulation, the tissue fluids and body secretions. These antibodies then bind to the antigens that stimulated their production in the first place. This antibody binding

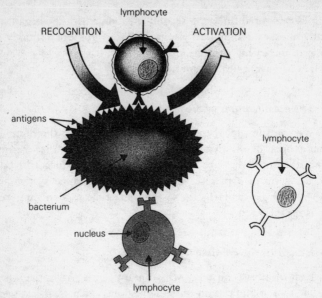

Fig. 3. A lymphocyte recognizes an antigen on a germ and becomes activated. Lymphocytes that do not recognize do not become activated.

has several consequences that eliminate or help to eliminate the germ. First antibody clumps germs together, which makes them easier to remove. Antibody also greatly increases the rate at which white blood cells can eat up germs. It can also kill germs directly, and finally it can coat and neutralize poisonous substances. So antibody is very versatile in getting rid of antigens. The other important type of lymphocyte is the T lymphocyte. It recognizes antigen and becomes stimulated in much the same way as the B lymphocyte, but does not make antibody. Instead its activated daughter cells have a number of other ways of getting rid of antigen. Firstly, they can attack and kill germs directly, or they can kill cells that have become infected with certain germs like viruses. They can also kill some abnormal cells and foreign 'outsider' cells. This is important in the rejection of organ transplants and might be important in some forms of cancer. Finally, T lymphocytes are crucial in overall control of immune responses.

How does this work in the body?

Where exactly is the immune system in the body? The answer is that it is everywhere. All our tissues contain millions of scavenger white blood cells and lymphocytes and are bathed in tissue fluid which contains antibodies. These cells are released into the blood stream from the bone marrow where they are made (Fig. 4).

From the blood stream they leave via the capillaries (the network of very tiny blood vessels present in all tissues) and migrate and meander through the tissues. In the normal course of events they then enter the lymph glands (the glands that swell up when we have an infection). From here both types of cell return to the blood stream, and then repeat the circuit.

These pathways mean that there is a continuous patrol by billions of lymphocytes and scavenger white blood cells going on through all our body tissues all the time. No bit of us is exempt from this security system. So the immune system essentially consists of a mobile army of security-conscious lymphocytes on constant patrol. If they identify an antigen, they respond by stopping in their tracks, sounding the alarm, initiating an immune response and

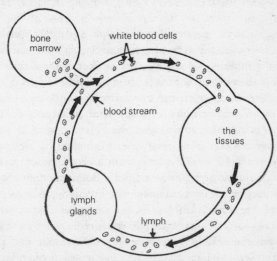

Fig. 4.   The circulation of white blood cells through the body.

summoning reinforcements. It is this astonishingly versatile and efficient system that maintains us in good health most of the time and allows us to recover from most infections relatively unscathed.

*How our understanding of the immune system
has changed our lives*

In 1798 Edward Jenner, a country general practitioner, performed the first immunization to protect against smallpox. He noticed that milkmaids who developed cowpox, which was a mild illness caught from cows, did not develop smallpox during epidemics. He took infected material from a cowpox sore and inoculated it into someone's skin, where it produced a small spot or pustule. Individuals who were vaccinated in this way did not develop smallpox during epidemics. How did it work? Smallpox and cowpox are both diseases which are caused by very similar viruses. In fact they share a common antigen but differ in virulence. Cowpox is a mild illness in man but smallpox is often fatal. Exposure to the cowpox virus at vaccination stimulates the immune system to produce antibody that can neutralize the cowpox virus. But this antibody also neutralizes smallpox virus because of the shared antigen. This is the general principle of all immunizations, which basically introduce killed or non-virulent bacteria or viruses to an individual's immune system so that antibody is produced. This antibody is then available to tackle the live virulent infection when it is encountered. After the success of Jenner's work with smallpox, the idea of vaccination quickly became widespread and was rapidly applied to many other infectious diseases.

Many diseases have now been eliminated or almost completely controlled by mass immunization programmes, including: smallpox, tetanus, diphtheria and polio. Immunization also gives good protection against tuberculosis, typhoid, cholera, yellow fever, and hepatitis B. In fact it is no exaggeration to say that modern immunization has radically improved our lives and greatly added to social stability, by removing the scourge of so many infectious diseases which used to kill large numbers of children and young people. But there are many remaining infectious diseases against which we would very much like effective immunization, and much research effort is currently being put into this. Our lives would be further improved if we could immunize against colds and 'flu, venereal diseases like herpes, syphilis, and gonorrhoea; tropical diseases like schistosomiasis and malaria; and of course, AIDS. There are fundamental problems that have so far prevented the development of vaccines against these diseases, but hopefully, as our understanding of the immune system increases, vaccines will eventually be developed to combat these diseases as well.

Problems in immunology

There are times when our immune system fails us or even makes mistakes, as it does in allergy. By failing to respond, or responding inappropriately, it can even cause disease rather than prevent it. So let us finish this review by looking at situations where it breaks down and leads to disease.

When the immune system is absent or damaged

There is a very rare congenital condition where the immune system fails to develop altogether. In this condition, which is called severe combined immunodeficiency (SCID), the bone marrow fails to make lymphocytes altogether. This is a fatal condition where the young infant will die rapidly of overwhelming infection. The only hope of a cure is by a bone marrow transplant. In another rare congenital condition the B lymphocytes do not develop properly, so that no antibody is produced. Children with this condition get repeated severe infections. This can be treated by giving regular injections of pooled antibody (antibody collected from many different blood donors and pooled together). Many other factors can damage the immune system and make us more prone to infections. These include malnutrition, vitamin deficiency and some chronic infections themselves. But these have to be fairly severe to have an effect. Our immune systems are remarkably resilient, and a well balanced sensible diet contains all the nutrients, including vitamins, required for good health. Additional vitamins are probably not necessary if you are on a normal diet. The immune systems of the very young and the very old are not always as efficient as at other times of life, making these two groups particularly prone to infection. Some cancers, particularly those of the lymph glands and the leukaemias, are very damaging to the immune response, as are some of the treatments used in cancer, such as radiotherapy, chemotherapy and high doses of steroid drugs. The most dramatic example of what happens when the immune system is destroyed is without doubt the acquired immunodeficiency syndrome (AIDS). This is caused by a new virus called HIV – the human immunodeficiency virus (previously called HTLV 3). This virus infects and then kills some sorts of T lymphocytes. Gradually the entire T lymphocyte population is wiped out, so that no immune responses can be initiated. This disease seems to be a completely new sort of infection in man, and was first noticed in homosexuals in New York and San Francisco in 1978. Since then more and more cases have been identified, so that it has now reached sufficient proportions to cause great concern. Thousands have now died of the disease in the USA. Early symptoms of AIDS are fever, weight loss, and enlargement of the lymph glands. Later on, as the immune system folds up completely, a most unusual form of cancer develops in some of the cases. This is called Kaposi's sarcoma. In the majority of the other cases, severe and often fatal infections occur. These infections are unusual in that they are caused by various germs that rarely, if ever, cause infections in healthy individuals. AIDS shows us just how important T lymphocytes are in keeping us free from overwhelming infections. The AIDS virus is quite difficult to catch – it is usually caught during sexual intercourse or by injection of the virus into the blood-stream. This is why in Europe and the USA the disease was confined to homosexuals (70 per cent of the cases) and their sexual partners, intravenous drug users, haemophiliacs, and babies of female AIDS victims, although it is now appearing in heterosexuals as well. In central Africa, AIDS is present in the heterosexual population. One way or another, all these groups catch the infection when the virus is introduced directly into the blood stream, from the blood or body secretions of an HIV carrying person.

Where we would like the immune system to do more

About twenty years ago there were great hopes that it might be possible to manipulate the immune system to help fight cancer, but unfortunately these hopes have not been fulfilled. Normal tissues and organs are made up of cells which work in a harmonious and organized way, generally speaking, for the benefit of the organism as a whole. Occasionally a rogue cell starts dividing in a disorganized and uncontrolled way to form abnormal cells, which disrupt the organ or tissues in which they arise and then spread to other organs and tissues, where they cause similar disruption and eventual death of the individual. This is basically what cancer is. In experimental cancers produced in laboratory animals, it was found that when the uncontrolled rogue cell started dividing, new antigens appeared on its surface. Now perhaps if the immune system could recognize these new antigens, an immune response could start against the cancer and lead to its rejection. Perhaps even vaccines against these antigens could be used to immunize people against various types of cancer. It was even suggested that one of the main roles of the immune system, besides protecting us from infection, was to protect us from cancer by spotting and eliminating new antigens on cancerous cells early on in their development. As things have turned out, the immune system is probably not all that important in stopping cancers from developing. There are two reasons for this. First of all, in people who have a very unhealthy immune system, there is no sudden overwhelming increase in the common forms of cancer like lung cancer or cancer of the breast, bowel and skin. For example, AIDS patients do not get these cancers. Secondly, most of the common forms of cancer in man do not, after all, seem to have new antigens on their surfaces. Where there is no antigen, there can be no immune response (this is a basic rule of immunology). So we would like the immune system to do more about cancer, but it is unlikely that this will be achieved as the common cancers just do not seem to have the necessary new antigens.

Transplants – the other side of the coin

When a surgeon transplants an organ, such as the kidney, or the heart, the immune system gets in the way.

The antigens on the cells of the new organ are immediately recognized as foreign 'outsiders', and a violent immune response leads to rejection of the organ. This rejection is the single greatest reason why transplants have been fraught with problems. The tendency for rejection can be reduced by matching the antigens of the donor organ as far as possible to those of the recipient. The closest possible match is to receive an organ transplant from an identical twin, in this case the antigens of donor and recipient are identical. Few of us have identical twins, so donor organs and potential recipients have to be tissue typed in the laboratory so that as close a match as possible can be achieved. But there is always some difference between donor and recipient, so organ transplant recipients have to be treated with drugs that suppress the immune system and prevent an immune response against the donor organ. The trouble with suppressing the immune response is that there is a risk of serious or even fatal infection. A careful balancing act has to be done to suppress the immune system just enough to prevent rejection, but not too much to allow fatal infections to develop. This is often possible, so that kidney transplants are now almost routine and the outlook is generally good. Hopefully, as experience grows, good results will also be achieved with heart, liver, and heart-lung transplants.

The enemy within

We said earlier that one of the main features of the immune system was its ability to distinguish between 'insiders' and 'outsiders'. Sometimes, however, the system seems to lose this ability and starts reacting to inside antigens on our own cells and tissues, resulting in severe damage to various tissues and organs. This is essentially a self-destructive act – 'the enemy within' – and these diseases can be very serious. No one yet knows why or how they develop, but fortunately they are quite rare. Examples of these diseases are certain types of thyroid disease, some kinds of diabetes, and haemolytic anaemia, where antibody attacks the red blood cells. Another type of disease is where several tissues and organs are attacked together by antibody. Rheumatoid arthritis is a fairly common example.

Allergy – at last

The final example of where the immune system works against us rather than for us is, of course, with the allergic response. Allergic reactions are immune reactions, but instead of protecting us they give us symptoms, and, as far as we can see, provide no useful function at all. Having now looked at how the immune system works as a whole, we can turn to what an allergic reaction is, how it works and what triggers it off.

Chapter Three

The Allergic Response.
The Immune System Gets It Wrong

In this chapter we will see exactly what the allergic reaction is, how it produces the symptoms of allergy, and, finally, some theories as to why we develop allergies in the first place, as they serve no useful function.

As we have said, allergic reactions are all immune reactions that do not protect but in fact cause damage by producing unnecessary symptoms. Allergic reactions are always directed against substances that are quite harmless in themselves, unlike the useful immune reactions that are directed against germs. It is the allergic reaction itself that is harmful. Pollen grains, house dust, cow's milk and cats are all in themselves quite innocuous and pass unnoticed by non-allergic people.

The allergic response works in just the same way as any immune response. Firstly, lymphocytes recognize an antigen. (In the case of allergy the antigen is called an allergen. 'Allergen' is just jargon for an antigen that happens to provoke an allergic response.) The stimulated lymphocytes then divide rapidly to form cells that make antibody that can bind on to the allergen that stimulated the response. So allergies are just as precisely targeted as any other immune reaction. This means that we can be allergic to just one type of grass pollen and not to another.

Allergy and atopy

The two words you may hear doctors use a lot are allergy and atopy. As we have said, allergy (Greek: *allos*, other; *ergon*, work) is the altered reactivity of a person so that he differs from normal people, as far as his response to a particular substance is concerned; he responds to it whereas others do not. People who have allergies are often called atopic. An atopic person has an abnormal state of reactivity or hypersensitivity to a substance. The two words boil down to very much the same thing for our purposes, namely, some people have a tendency to develop allergies to various things (pollen, etc.) when exposed to them (become sensitized), whereas the majority of people do not develop these reactions. This predisposition to get allergies is, to an extent, genetically determined, that is, allergies tend to run in families. And there is wide variation in range and extent of allergies between people. Some people have an allergy to just one thing, others are allergic to lots. Generally speaking, if you have a very severe allergy to something you are likely to have allergies to several other things as well. Incidentally, allergies don't just crop up in humans but happen to other species as well. For example, cats and dogs get allergies too, so pet-lovers take note!

The way allergy works

There are two phases: first, the setting up of the allergic response or 'sensitization', which leaves a person allergic to something, and second, the triggering leading to an attack when that person meets the allergen again. Sensitization can happen when an allergen lands on a surface from which it is absorbed (Fig. 5).

The surface can be the skin, the moist mucous membrane lining of the nose, mouth or lungs, or the lining of the digestive system – all common areas affected by allergy. The allergen is then recognized by a lymphocyte, and large amounts of a special form of antibody called IgE are made.

IgE is the major antibody of allergy. This is because it can stick on to special cells called mast cells, which we will come to in a moment. As soon as mast cells are coated in IgE antibody the scene is set for allergic reactions and that person is said to be sensitized. Once sensitized, that person will have an allergic attack when he or she meets the allergen again. A person with hayfever may start sneezing seconds after pollen grains land in the nose, and

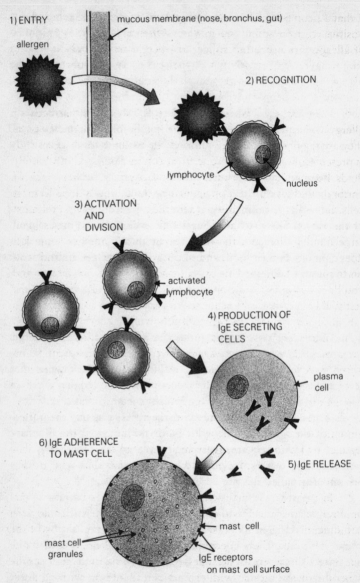

1) ENTRY

allergen

mucous membrane (nose, bronchus, gut)

2) RECOGNITION

lymphocyte

nucleus

3) ACTIVATION AND DIVISION

activated lymphocyte

4) PRODUCTION OF IgE SECRETING CELLS

plasma cell

6) IgE ADHERENCE TO MAST CELL

5) IgE RELEASE

mast cell

mast cell granules

IgE receptors on mast cell surface

Fig. 5.   Setting up of an allergy – 'sensitization'.

if that person had a skin test with pollen extract, there would be a positive reaction within two minutes. Often only very tiny amounts of allergen are needed to trigger an allergic attack.

IgE

We must say a bit more about IgE, the special antibody of allergy which sticks to mast cells. People become allergic because they are good at making IgE antibody in response to allergens. IgE is present only in very low concentrations in blood and other body fluids because it sticks to mast cells so quickly. Other types of antibody that give protection against germs do not stick on to mast cells. IgE is made mainly just where the allergen gets in, and most of the IgE sticks on to local mast cells which are also present in large numbers beneath the mucous membrane linings. Some IgE does circulate in the blood, and so can reach distant parts and stick on to mast cells there. This explains why if you have hayfever and you have a skin test done on your forearm with pollen extract, the test will be positive. The sequence of events here is that anti-pollen IgE antibody is made in the nose following inhalation of pollen. Some of this IgE passes to distant tissues in the blood, including the forearm skin, where it sticks to mast cells and sensitizes them. When pollen extract is put into the skin of the forearm, the IgE-sensitized mast cells trigger the reaction.

Two final facts about IgE; normal people have very low levels in the blood, but people with allergies tend to have raised amounts. Secondly, people with parasitic infections such as intestinal worms often have very high levels in the blood. We will return to this interesting point when we talk about why people become allergic at all.

In 1921 two German scientists, Prausnitz and Kustner, did an important experiment which showed that allergic reactions were due to something in blood serum. Kustner had an allergy to fish. Some of his serum was injected into the skin of Prausnitz, who did not have fish allergy. When the area of skin injected with serum was subsequently tested with fish extract, there was a strong positive reaction, but when adjacent skin was tested, it was negative.

This showed that there was something in the serum of Kustner that sensitized the skin of Prausnitz to fish. Now we know that this substance was IgE. In the 1921 experiment, Kustner's anti-fish specific IgE had sensitized the skin mast cells of Prausnitz to fish extract. His skin had then shown an immediate hypersensitivity reaction to fish.

Mast cells: what are they?

Mast cells contain many granules and are present in most organs, but they are particularly concentrated at the surface mucous membranes (the lining of the digestive system, nose and lungs and the skin). When a mast cell is covered in IgE antibody, it will be triggered whenever an allergen arrives that precisely fits that antibody. Triggering happens when the IgE antibody molecules are cross-linked or bridged by the allergen (Fig. 6).

This leads to activation and the granules in the cell are then released. These granules contain many different substances collectively called 'mediators', because they mediate inflammation.

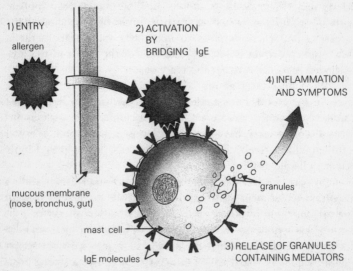

Fig. 6.   Triggering of mediator release from sensitized mast cells by allergen.

These mediators have several different effects, but generally they produce allergic inflammation and so are responsible for the symptoms of allergy. They act as follows.

First, they increase the blood supply to the region where the mast cells have been activated and make the capillary blood vessels leaky so that there is an outpouring of fluid from the blood stream into the affected area. This produces the symptoms of inflammation with swelling, redness, heat and discomfort. It also brings white blood cells and antibody from the blood stream into the affected area. The symptoms resulting will depend on where this reaction happens, but can include itching, sneezing, coughing, red eyes, sore throat and so on. Their second important effect is to stimulate mucous glands in the surface mucous membrane leading to an outpouring of fluid, and again the symptoms depend on the affected area and can include running nose and watering eyes. The third effect is that they make the smooth muscle layer which lines the bronchi go into a state of contraction. This is important in the production of allergic asthma, as muscle spasm narrows the bronchi, producing breathlessness and wheeze. This will be discussed in greater detail in Chapter 5. At the moment, an enormous amount of research is being devoted to these mast cell mediators. As they become more precisely understood, it will be possible to develop new drugs to block their effects and so more effectively to relieve the symptoms of allergy. Of course we already have several effective anti-allergy drugs.

One of the best known of the allergy mediators is histamine. Antihistamines have been used for years for hayfever, and in many cases they are very effective. They work by preventing the allergic inflammation due to histamine in the nose and throat. The fact that antihistamines are not effective against all allergies (for example, they are of little use in asthma) is due to the many other mast cell mediators of allergy which are important and are not blocked by antihistamines. Another anti-allergy drug, called sodium cromoglycate, is thought to work in part by blocking release of granules from triggered mast cells. As research progresses, it is becoming clear that mediators are very complex and have many different roles in different situations. Just before leaving mast cells, we must stress that sometimes they are triggered to release granules without being activated by IgE and allergen. Some other things can 'destabilize' them and produce allergic-type symptoms where no allergen is involved. We will return to this later.

Eosinophils

Another type of white blood cell may be involved in allergy, but quite how is not clear. Eosinophils are present in the blood stream in low numbers in normal people. In allergy the numbers are often greatly raised. This can be detected by a simple blood test and can indicate that a condition may be allergic. One of the functions of the eosinophil may be to 'clean up' after an allergic reaction by sucking in spent antibody and mediators.

Allergens – the cause of allergy

So what sorts of things cause allergies? In other words, what is it about some substances that makes them into allergens and able to trigger off IgE antibody production and so lead to allergy? Only relatively few of all the antigens there are can act as allergens, and why this is so remains a mystery. But allergens have a few things in common. First, they have to be able to dissolve in water. Second, after dissolving in watery secretions they have to be small enough to get through the mucous membrane of the nose, lung or digestive system, but not so small that they are swept away in the blood stream and so never meet a lymphocyte to trigger an allergy. Third, they have to be around in the environment. They have to be commonly available. Even so, this does not explain why some substances are so troublesome and are common causes of allergy, whereas others, often more plentiful, pass largely unnoticed.

Allergens can be divided up into groups. First there are those that are 'intermittent'. We only encounter them from time to time, for example a food that we only eat now and again like strawberries or shellfish. Second are the seasonal allergens – these are mainly pollens and fungal spores that are present everywhere, but only for part of the year. Finally there are allergens that are with us all the year round, the perennial allergens like house dust.

Allergens can also be grouped according to how they get into the body. They can be inhaled, eaten, come in contact with our skin, or be injected. The main allergens are listed in Table 1 on pages 46–7. How much allergen is needed to cause sensitization? No one really knows. How much is required to trigger an attack in a sensitized person? This depends of course on how allergic they have become, but certainly very tiny amounts may be enough.

The symptoms allergens produce, as we have said, are largely determined by how they enter the body. So by and large, inhaled allergens lead to rhinitis and asthma, allergens that contact the skin lead to various skin rashes, and allergens that are eaten lead to digestive problems. Allergens may also trigger other unusual symptoms.

The inhaled allergens

Airborne substances are the most plentiful, and by far the commonest cause of allergy overall. At least 10 per cent of the population have an allergy to some inhaled allergen or other.

POLLEN

Pollen is by far the commonest inhaled allergen, and the most frequent allergy it causes is hayfever. There may be as many as 5 million hayfever sufferers in the UK. Pollen is a seasonal allergen, but why is it so common? Wind-pollenated plants produce billions of small pollen grains which travel vast distances with ease in the air. This is the pollen that causes the trouble and it comes from trees, grasses and weeds. The heavier, rather sticky, less plentiful pollen which colourful flowers produce, relying on insects to do the pollenating, is less troublesome, though allergy can develop to this pollen, particularly when flowers are cut and put indoors. During the hayfever season, pollen is pretty well impossible to avoid. It is everywhere, so that the number of people with hayfever gives an indication of the number of people who are actually

Table 1: Allergens

INHALED ALLERGENS

1 POLLEN

Trees

Birch	Ash	
Plane	Elm	
Beech	Oak	
Hazel	Maple	
Sycamore	Walnut	
Alder	Olive	
Willow		

Grasses

Timothy
Rye
Bermuda (hot climates)

Weeds

Nettle	Plantain
Mugwort	Ragweed (USA)

Flowers

e.g. the Compositae family

2 DUSTS

(a) House dust (a complex mix of things)
House dust mite excreta in house dust

(b) Other dusts: sawdust
dust from grain and flour
dust from hay

3 ANIMALS

Cat	Hamster	Rabbit	Wool (sheep)
Dog	Rat	Horse	Feather (birds)
Guinea pig	Mouse	Cow	? other humans

4 FUNGAL SPORES

Cladosporium	*Serpua lacrymans*	*Phoma*
Alternaria	(dry rot)	*Pullularia*
Penicillium	*Fusarium*	*Mucor*
Aspergillus	*Sporobolomyces*	*Candida*
Rhizopus	*Botrytis*	*Helminthosporium*

5 OTHER

(a) Chemicals:
Airfresheners
Insecticides
Pine resin colophony used in solder flux
Agents used in plastic manufacture
Fumes from cavity wall insulation

(b) Other insects:
Insect debris from silverfish and cockroaches
Mites in grain and flour
Locusts

INGESTED ALLERGENS

Foods	*Additives*	*Drugs*
Milk	Preservatives	e.g. antibiotics
Cereal	Antioxidants	
Yeast	Colouring agents	
Egg	Flavouring	
Nuts		
Strawberries		
Fish		

CONTACT ALLERGENS

(a) Plants: primula, begonia, chrysanthemum, poison ivy (USA only)
(b) Clothing: cotton, other fabrics, shoes, leather, rubber
(c) Drugs: in ointments and creams
(d) Cleaning agents: soap, shampoo, detergents, washing powder, enzyme-containing washing powder
(e) Cosmetics: powders and creams, perfumes, hairsprays, deodorant, aftershave, bleaching agents, hairdyes, etc.
(f) Metals and jewellery: nickel, mercury, chromium
(g) Chemicals: paints, polishes, castor seed oil, cotton seed oil, inks

INJECTED ALLERGENS

(a) 'Natural' injections: bees, wasps, hornets, other insects
(b) 'Man-made' injections: of drugs, e.g., antibiotics, antitetanus serum

capable of becoming allergic in a given community. Exposure to many other allergens is limited to groups of people in certain environments. For example, not everyone is exposed to horses or cats.

The types of pollen that are around at any time vary from one geographical region to another and obviously depend on the plants of that region. Plants pollenate in a predictable sequence according to season. People with allergies to particular pollens will then develop symptoms of hayfever or asthma during that plant's pollenation period. In temperate climates, tree pollens usually appear first. In the UK, most trees pollenate in March and April and the tree pollen season is quite short. Generally, allergy to tree pollen causes less trouble than allergy to grass pollen, as it is less plentiful.

Grasses pollenate during May, June and July, and these are the problem months for hayfever victims. This is not only because grass produces lots of pollen, but because there is a vast amount of grass around, even in the inner city. Grass covers huge amounts of the earth's surface. The pollen grains of grass are just the right size to land in the nose and eyes, which is where the worst symptoms usually are. They can also reach the lung and lead to asthma. In temperate zones, timothy and rye grass are common. In hot climates, Bermuda grass is common. Up to a dozen different sorts of grass are responsible for hayfever in the UK.

In July and August, the weeds pollenate. They do not cause as much trouble in the UK as grass pollen allergy. Nettle, mugwort and plantain are the common ones. But in the USA, ragweed is a very common cause of allergy. It has been estimated that about a quarter of a million tons of ragweed pollen is released into the air in the USA during its pollenation season. No wonder ragweed allergy is so common in the USA.

The exact timing of pollen seasons depends on climatic variations, so the pollen season for grass can be late or early, depending on the weather. The weather also has a day-to-day effect on the amount of pollen around. A sudden downpour in June will lower the amount of pollen around and bring temporary relief to the hayfever sufferer. Hayfever symptoms are usually worst when the count is high. During the summer months, the pollen count is published daily in the papers. This is measured in a machine that sucks air past a sticky microscope slide. The pollen is trapped on this and the grains are then counted under the miscroscope.

HOUSE DUST

After pollen, house dust is probably the next most common airborne allergen. House dust is a mixture of things: it includes fibres from fabrics in the house like wool from carpets and blankets, particles of soil brought in from outside, carbon soot and other atmospheric pollutants deposited from the air, particles of dirt, food, debris from insects, animal fur, skin scales and so on. People may be allergic to one or to several things in this complex mix, but the strongest and most common allergen in house dust is the excreta of the house dust mite.

THE HOUSE DUST MITE (*Dermatophagoides pteronysinus*)

This peculiar little insect measures about one third of a millimetre and eats human skin scales. Its life span is about five months. It lives in beds, pillows, mattresses, and to a lesser extent in carpets, curtains and soft furnishings. It loves warm moist human environments and hates extreme cold. As the mite is with us all year long, and as we spend about a third of our time in bed, people who become allergic will have symptoms all the year round, most commonly rhinitis and asthma. In fact the excreta of the house dust mite is the most important cause of perennial rhinitis (that is, symptoms like hayfever all the year round) in the western world. It is not so common in hot climates, where there are fewer carpets and soft furnishings. In fact, people who immigrate from hot climates to the UK quite often develop allergies shortly after arrival. The mite is very difficult to get rid of, short of fumigating the bedroom. It resists most ordinary insecticides. Vacuum cleaning can reduce the numbers of mites, but this may not help the very allergic. Removal of fitted carpets and use of foam rubber mattresses may help. Other sorts of mite can infest stored cereals and flour and give allergies to those who work with them.

ANIMALS AND PETS

The third important group of inhaled allergens comes from animals. The actual allergen is usually in the animal's skin scales which, being very light, become airborne and are easily inhaled. Allergy is also possible to animal hair, and to the urine of some animals, in particular cats and rats. Allergy can develop to pretty well any furry animal if you are exposed to it. Allergy to lions may be a problem for liontamers! But in the home, the common culprits are cats, dogs, guinea pigs, hamsters and rabbits. Animals at work can cause problems. Laboratory workers exposed to rats or mice can develop serious symptoms that may mean changing jobs. Jockeys who become allergic to horses may have hard decisions to make as well. Children who are given pets often have very close contact with them, providing easy opportunity for sensitization. Allergy to animals can be exquisite, so that a severe attack may be triggered in a cat-allergic person who enters a room vacated by a cat the day before. Humans shed skin scales as well, and it has been suggested that some people can actually be allergic to other people, but this has not yet been proved. More rarely, allergy can develop to wool and feathers. This will mean a change in bedding.

MOULDS AND SPORES

The last big group of inhaled allergens comes from fungi. Fungi thrive on damp rotten vegetation or in damp housing. Fungal spores are the seeds, and are light like pollen but smaller, so they tend not to cause eye problems. Spores are present most of the year but are most plentiful in the autumn. Those allergic to fungi often have their worst symptoms then. Among the most common are *Cladosporium* and *Alternaria*, which live indoors and outdoors and peak in the early autumn. In damp houses, *Penicillium* (mildew) and *Cladosporium* can thrive on, for example, wallpaper. Dry rot spores from fruiting bodies are confined to houses with serious woodwork problems, and *Aspergillus*, an important fungus as we shall see later, likes rotting vegetation. How important are these fungi as causes of allergy? As yet there is no clear answer to this question, but between 4 and 20 per cent of allergy patients have a positive skin test to a fungus, and there is some evidence that some cases of seasonal asthma may be due to fungal allergy. Those with allergies to fungal spores are usually most troubled in the autumn, and least troubled in January, February and March. Unlike plant pollen, humid or wet weather encourages spore-release, so that those with fungal allergy may find that they are worse on wet days. Obviously damp houses do not suit those with allergy to fungi, although generally there are less fungal spores indoors than out.

The allergens we eat

First, there are the natural components of our diet. The commonest allergies are to milk, cereals, fish, eggs, yeast, nuts and soft fruit. Second, there is increasing concern about allergy to food additives, the colourings, flavourings and anti-oxidants that are being increasingly used in processed food. Finally, allergies can develop to drugs and medicines. These interesting issues will all be dealt with in detail later.

Contactants

Our skin, eyes, mouth and hands come into contact with a bewildering range of different substances, many of which can provoke allergies. The more common ones are listed in the table and, again, we will deal with them in greater detail later. For the moment, the ones that can cause particular trouble are cosmetics, detergents, jewellery, hairdye, perfumes and deodorants.

Other allergens

These are a mixed bag of other substances that cause trouble from time to time. Injections of insect venom directly into the body from bees and wasps, or drugs and medicines from doctors can occasionally give serious allergic reactions. Unusual substances may be encountered in the work place and lead to allergy. These are mainly various chemicals not normally encountered.

Rare forms of allergy

To be complete, we must mention one or two other ways in which allergy can arise. Most allergies are due to IgE antibody directed against an allergen. Sometimes, people make other sorts of antibody to an allergen. When they meet the allergen again, they have different sorts of allergic reactions. These conditions are fairly rare. Here are two examples. When injections of horse serum were used a lot in medicine, some people became allergic to the serum so that when they had a second injection they became ill with fever and joint pains. This condition was appropriately called 'serum sickness'. The second example of unusual allergic responses is the condition called 'farmer's lung', where some farmers develop an allergy to the fungal spores present in mouldy hay. A few hours after exposure to the hay they develop cough, fever and breathlessness. A similar sort of illness can affect people who breed pigeons – 'pigeon-fancier's lung'.

Another form of allergy affects the skin. In Chapter 2 we saw that some immune reactions do not involve antibody at all, but, rather, that the T lymphocytes responded directly with the antigen and produced a reaction. In the condition of contact dermatitis, it is the T lymphocytes and not antibody in the skin that cause the reaction and produce allergic symptoms and skin rash. Because these reactions are due to T lymphocytes, they take longer to develop. They are usually called 'delayed hypersensitivity reactions'.

Are allergies inherited?

The tendency to develop allergies is definitely in the genes, but the inheritance is complex and many factors seem to be involved. In one study the child of two allergic parents had a 75 per cent chance of being allergic; if one parent was allergic then the child had a 50 per cent chance. But having an allergic parent is not essential. About 40 per cent of all allergy sufferers have neither parent affected by allergy, and, conversely, allergic parents do not always have allergic children.

Why do allergies arise?

A further question of great interest is why some people get allergies and others do not. Why does the immune system make this mistake? This remains a mystery, but if we could answer this question it could open the door to finding a cure. We have already said that we all have mast cells and the capacity to make IgE, so that we all have the potential to become sensitized to allergens, yet most of us never do. To put it the other way round, we can consider the allergic individual as someone who has an ability to identify and respond to what are often very tiny doses of allergens presented to the surface of a mucous membrane or the skin. Could this ability have any advantage to an individual? Perhaps the allergic response is really part of a protective immune response. Individuals who have parasitic infestations of the gut with, for example, worms usually have high levels of IgE antibody to these parasites; this leads to an inflammatory reaction on the mucous membranes where the worms are attached, which may damage the parasites and protect the individual against them. In fact it has been suggested that the IgE antibody/mast cell system is well suited to help clear the surface of the digestive system, the lung, nose and the skin of worms and other parasites that can live on these surfaces, as the allergic inflammatory response produces symptoms which promote clearing. Itching of the skin and scratching, coughing, sneezing, running of the nose, diarrhoea and vomiting will help wash parasites away. In parts of the world where people frequently have infestations by all sorts of parasitic worms, the allergic reaction may be important in preventing overwhelming and possibly fatal infections. In the developed parts of the world, where social hygiene has virtually eliminated parasites, the allergic response may be basically redundant. But we continue to notice the allergic response when it responds to normally harmless substances like pollen grains or dust.

Another interesting possibility has been suggested. This is that allergy might protect against cancer. If this could be proved, it would obviously be very exciting. Several studies have been done to see if allergic people get less cancer than others. Some suggest that this is so, whereas others do not. So it must be emphasized that there is no convincing evidence whatever at the moment that allergy protects against cancer, important though such an association would be.

A third suggestion to explain allergy is simply that it is just a side-effect of having an immune system at all and, as allergic diseases are rarely fatal, there is no selective disadvantage for the allergic individual, so that allergies just persist in the population.

How do allergies arise?

Allergies tend to run in families. But this does not explain why one person gets an allergy and another does not, when both are exposed to allergens. There is no full answer to this question yet, but an interesting suggestion has been made. We have already mentioned IgE antibody, which is responsible for allergy. One of the other types of antibody that we all produce is called IgA. This antibody is present in the secretions (saliva, tears, mucus) that bathe the mucous membranes. It is thought to be of importance in neutralizing germs and poisonous substances before they get an opportunity to invade. Sometimes, particularly in the very young, there is far less IgA than normal. This lack of IgA may increase the chance of allergy. The way this works could be that lack of IgA at the surface of the mucous membrane means that allergens, instead of being mopped up, are able to penetrate the mucous membrane and so stimulate IgE antibody, and therefore allergy. Many studies have been done to try and prove this, but results are conflicting so the theory is unproven as yet.

Another theory to explain allergy is based on control mechanisms in the immune response. The immune system is controlled by the T lymphocytes, of which there are several sorts. Some turn immune reactions on, and others turn them off. It may be that the 'turning-off' lymphocytes are important in preventing us all being allergic, as they stop us reacting to allergens. If they are disturbed, possibly by virus infections, they are unable to prevent us responding to an allergen and so we become allergic.

Age and other factors in allergy

Allergy can develop for the first time at any age, but most allergy starts in childhood. As we grow older so does the immune system, and it gets less efficient in responding. This is why old people often get serious infections. Generally, as we get older we get less allergic. Children and adolescents often 'grow out' of their allergies, although an unlucky few carry their allergies into adulthood. At the other end of the age spectrum, babies during the first three months of life can get food allergies quite easily. This may be because the baby's digestive system is immature and allows allergens to penetrate. It has been shown that bottle-fed babies are more likely to develop eczema and cow's milk allergy than their breast-fed counterparts. Another effect that age has is that it seems to alter the pattern of allergies. Allergic infants often have eczema and colic. The allergic five-year-old often has nasal problems, and the older child with allergy often has asthma and hayfever.

The effects of climate, temperature, humidity and geographical location on allergy are well known, and have the influences they do by largely determining the variety and amount of allergen in the environment at any particular time. Climate determines plant life and therefore pollenation and sporulation seasons, which in turn determine the variety of pollen and spore allergens present in the air at any time. In temperate climates, grass pollen largely determines the hayfever season, but no country, regardless of climate, is totally pollen-free. Probably the most allergen-free environment is to be found in an Alpine village in the winter. Here, the vegetation is covered by snow so that there is little, if any, pollen. There is no urban atmosphere pollution and little dust, and the cold dry atmosphere minimizes the growth of fungi and moulds. It is of course well known that allergy sufferers often improve in the Alps. The other way you can get away from it all is by taking an ocean cruise.

The effect of stress on allergy is complicated. One reason for this is that stress is difficult to measure and comes in so many shapes and forms. As a broad generalization, many allergy sufferers notice that their condition gets worse under stress and this seems particularly true of asthma.

Can allergies be prevented?

In theory all you have to do is avoid the allergen. In practice this is easier said than done. Pollen and fungal spores are inescapable unless you live in a space suit and breathe specially filtered air. Even dust and the house dust mite are difficult to avoid, despite the most meticulous vacuum cleaning. If you are allergic to a pet the simple solution is to get rid of it, but this can be a major problem when it is a much loved and important member of the household. It is really only with the more unusual allergies that avoidance can work. It is quite easy to avoid strawberries, nuts or shellfish if these are the obvious cause of a particular allergy, but not so easy if the allergy is to cereals or dairy products which are present in so many foods. So, on the whole, the common allergies cannot easily be prevented by avoiding the allergen.

Chapter Four

The Range of Allergies and How They Can Be Detected

The spectrum of allergic disease and the organs affected

How can the basic allergic reaction produce so many different symptoms and disorders in many different organs, and how can this lead to the detection and diagnosis of an allergy? Pretty well any organ can be affected, but allergy strikes some more than others. These are sometimes called the 'shock' or 'target' organs. They are more vulnerable to allergic attack because they contain lots of IgE antibody-coated mast cells.

Sometimes just one organ is affected; for example, itching and watering of the nose may be the only symptom, as in hayfever. Or many organs may be involved; an infant who is allergic to cow's milk may get digestive system, skin and lung troubles, so that after a bottle feed, colic, asthma and eczema develop.

As so many organs can be affected by a variety of different symptoms, doctors from several specialities may be consulted, including family practitioner, chest specialist, dermatologist, gastro-enterologist, ophthalmologist, and ear, nose and throat specialist. In view of the widespread nature of allergy, the 'holistic' approach has been advocated, and, as we have already said, in the USA there is a separate medical speciality of allergy (sometimes called allergology).

Of course, the organ involved depends largely on where the allergen gets into the body. So the commonest allergies affect the nose and lungs because inhaled allergens are the most plentiful. Usually if the allergen is inhaled the symptoms only strike the respiratory system; if the allergen is eaten, they strike the digestive system; and if the allergen comes in contact with the skin, they strike the skin. But this is not always so. For instance, someone who is allergic to strawberries may develop wheezing and urticaria (itchy lumps) after eating them. This is because the allergen in the strawberries gets into the blood stream and travels round to the skin and lungs where it sticks to the anti-strawberry IgE coated mast cells. The main symptoms of airborne allergens are allergic conjunctivitis with itching and watering of the eyes, allergic rhinitis and hayfever with itching and sneezing, blocking and running of the nose and allergic asthma with wheezing, coughing and breathlessness. The throat and ear can also be involved, with itching and discomfort. Chronic severe cases may develop nasal polyps (swelling of the mucous membrane lining to the nose) which may permanently block the nose, and inflammation of the middle ear which can lead to deafness. Of all the respiratory allergies by far the commonest is hayfever, and only one in ten hayfever sufferers ever gets asthma.

The next 'shock' organ is the skin. Several common skin diseases can have an allergic basis, including eczema, which is a persistent red patchy rash that flakes, cracks and peels, and urticaria or 'hives', which usually comes in acute attacks of sudden itchy lumps which can resemble insect bites. The third major shock organ is the digestive system. Allergy in the digestive system can give many symptoms, including nausea and vomiting, abdominal pain and diarrhoea.

All the allergies, regardless of the organ affected (with the important exception of eczema), are largely due to the triggering of the mast cells by allergen. This leads to swelling and inflammation, starting within moments of contact with the allergen and reaching its height within a few minutes. This sudden immediate reaction sometimes goes on to a longer reaction which can last for hours or even days, which explains the long-lasting nature of the symptoms of chronic allergy.

The severity of allergies

This is very variable. Fortunately, most allergy sufferers have reasonably mild symptoms for only part of the year, so that their disability is limited. Less fortunate are those, often with multiple allergies, who have chronic severe symptoms all year round. Although a great nuisance and source of misery, allergies are rarely fatal and people who have them are usually completely healthy otherwise. A fortunately rare exception is anaphylaxis. This is a generalized, severe and potentially fatal allergic reaction that happens when a highly sensitized individual is exposed to an often fairly massive dose of allergen. This results in massive widespread triggering of mast cells, with very severe symptoms of flushing, wheezing and shock which can even lead to death.

The time factor

Allergies are unpredictable; they can develop at any age, although most start in the early years of life. They can come and go, clearing up spontaneously, or they can last a lifetime. No one can yet predict how any particular person's allergy is going to behave. Similarly, allergies can swap from one organ to another. The capricious nature of allergies should hearten the frustrated allergy victim, as there is at least always a chance that the allergy will simply vanish overnight for no apparent reason.

Time is important in allergy in another way. Most of us who are going to be allergy sufferers develop our first allergies early in life, and it is the first few months of life that may be important in determining what a particular individual may be allergic to. For example, the season in which a child is born may determine its allergies. In a study done in Finland it was shown that children born between February and April had an increased risk of allergy to birch pollen, that those born between April and May had an increased risk of allergy to grass pollen and mugwort, and that those born after July and August had the least risk of grass pollen allergy. It would seem that the first pollen season that a baby experiences can condition the pattern of allergy. In the UK, babies born between May and October have an increased chance of being allergic to house dust mite in later life. The timing of changes in environments may also be crucial. For instance, in the UK roughly 5 per cent of all school children have asthma (most have it either mildly or only very occasionally), as do West Indian children born in the UK. But of West Indian children born in the West Indies but living in the UK, fewer have asthma.

Unsolved,puzzles

No one knows why some people develop allergies and others do not. Certainly inheritance and genetics play a part, but this is not the whole story. The fact remains that only a small percentage of people who are exposed to a particular allergen ever develop an allergy to it. Another odd fact which we will be coming to shortly is that while between 30–40 per cent of the population have a positive skin test to some allergen or other, only 10–15 per cent have allergic symptoms. Why is this? No one knows. Why some infants get cow's milk allergy and some children get hayfever remains largely a mystery. Other puzzles abound. Why do some allergy sufferers switch the organ in which they develop symptoms? Why do some children oscillate between asthma and eczema, yet others have periods when both are troublesome.

In eczema there is the problem of identifying the allergen, because it is not known at the moment. Further difficulties remain. Many young dust mite allergic children, as determined by skin tests, have no symptoms at all, whereas others do. Why? Many young adults with eczema have high levels of IgE antibodies directed against house dust mite or grass pollen, and yet have no hayfever or asthma. Why? Finally, why do some people who have allergy to grass pollen get hayfever alone, yet others get asthma as well? As yet the answers to these questions are anybody's guess.

The detection and diagnosis of allergies

Some allergies are obvious. Many symptoms are absolutely characteristic and typical of an allergy. If I cross a meadow in mid June and ten minutes later I start sneezing violently, my nose pours and my eyes swell up and itch, it is pretty obvious that I have hayfever. Similarly, if after eating snails, which I rarely do, I come up in gigantic, red, itchy lumps all over, it is pretty obvious that I am allergic to them. Detecting the cause of allergy here is not a problem. The victim knows. There was contact with an allergen and symptoms developed. Doctors and sophisticated tests are quite unnecessary here. Avoid the allergen. The simple and obvious accounts for most allergy cases. It can be much more difficult though. There are the cases where exposure to the allergen, for example a food, is continuous. Here a more thorough and painstaking search for a cause may be required.

The patient's history

The actual details and timing of all the symptoms very often make the diagnosis of an allergy extremely likely. But it is important to be aware that some allergic-type symptoms can be caused by other disease processes as well. So it is most important, if you develop a symptom that persists for some time, not just to write it off as a tiresome allergy but go and discuss it with your doctor. The details of your symptoms will often point towards them being triggered by one of the common allergens. The time of day and the length of the symptoms, or the time of year when they are worst, will often point towards, for example, pollens, fungi, animals, plants, dust in the house, a substance encountered at work or doing a favourite hobby. There may be a clear reaction to a particular drug or food. Allergic symptoms may be dramatically altered by a trip abroad, staying with friends or moving house. A careful look at what is around you at home and at work may give you a valuable clue as to the cause of your allergy if it is not already obvious to you. Is the bedroom damp, dusty or poorly ventilated? Do you get better when you go on a trip and leave the cat at home? Are you much worse since buying that new mattress? Is your worst time during the spring or the autumn? Does a smoky atmosphere make matters worse? What is the effect of exercise or emotional stress on your symptoms? Taking note of all these points will help you to gain insight into what does and does not suit you and your allergy, and may go a long way towards providing you with a cure by avoiding the things that trigger your attacks – that is, if they are avoidable. Not all are, of course.

The doctor's examination

If you go and see a doctor, he will first take a detailed account of your symptoms along the lines we have mentioned, plus details of any other illnesses you may have had. He will then do a physical examination. This is very often completely normal, and this is when some allergy sufferers feel embarrassed as there is nothing to see for the severe and disabling symptoms that they have described. Don't worry. Doctors who are experienced in allergy are quite used to this. There is nothing quite like a visit to the doctor for the rash to vanish, the wheeze to go away or the nose to stop running. This is typical of allergic symptoms. They come and go, so there are times when there is nothing to see. Obviously it is very helpful if the doctor can see the rash or the red itchy eyes, but it is not essential. In the case of intermittent wheezing the doctor can give you a small meter to take home, on which you can measure your own breathing at different times of the day and so help to make the diagnosis.

What tests might the doctor do?

Quite often tests are unnecessary, as the allergy and its cause are obvious. This is just as well, as infants and little children are easily upset by tests.

The most simple and useful test for allergy is a skin test. This is done by putting a small drop of an extract of the substance suspected of causing the allergy on to the skin, usually the forearm, and then very gently pricking or scratching (so as not to draw blood) the surface of the skin. A small amount of the extract then seeps through to the lower layers of the skin. If a person is allergic to that extract, that is, has IgE antibody to it, then mast cells in the skin are triggered and a positive reaction is seen, with reddening, itching and swelling around the drop of extract, the characteristic weal and flare response. This develops within ten minutes of the test and looks a bit like an insect bite. It is usual to test people by using a battery of common allergen extracts, normally about twenty. A drop of each is put on the skin in a row, and then each is pricked into the skin using a separate needle for each so as not to mix up the different allergens. These are the grass and tree pollens, various fungi, cat, dog, horse, feathers, house dust and the house dust mite. A so called 'negative control' is done as well. This is just a drop of fluid without any allergen extract in it. This should not produce a reaction. Occasionally it does, as some individuals are very sensitive to minor skin trauma (dermatographism). A positive reaction to the negative control casts doubt on the other prick tests, as those that are positive may also just be due to this irritant effect. A 'positive control' is also done to ensure that the whole system is working. This is a solution of histamine (one of the mediators discussed earlier), which should always provoke a reaction in allergic and non-allergic people alike. The 'positive control' will be negative and so may the other skin tests if the patient is taking an antihistamine drug. You should stop taking antihistamines at least forty-eight hours before having skin tests, to prevent a 'false negative' result. Other drugs do not usually interfere with skin tests and can be continued.

The results of skin tests taken together with the history of symptoms can be very helpful in identifying and confirming the common allergies. Tests on their own do not mean very much. They must be taken together with the symptoms. They are particularly useful for identifying the airborne allergens responsible for hayfever, rhinitis and allergic asthma. Skin tests are quick, convenient, cheap and safe, but need to be done by an expert as the way they are done is important to getting reliable results. Skin tests are on the whole less helpful when it comes to food allergy. They are often positive with nut, fish and shellfish allergy, but are often negative in milk or grain and cereal allergy. Skin testing can also be used in special circumstances to identify more unusual allergies, for example, allergy to certain drugs like penicillin and some cases of allergy related to occupational exposure. For example, workers who refine platinum may develop asthma on exposure to platinum and have a positive skin test to platinum. Generally, skin tests are an exquisitely sensitive way of detecting allergies. In platinum allergy, it has been calculated that as little as 10^{-15} of a gram or 200,000 molecules of a platinum salt will produce a positive skin test.

There are, of course, some problems with skin tests. Firstly, 30–40 per cent of the general population of the UK and the USA have one or more positive tests to the standard battery of common allergens, yet only 10–15 per cent have any allergic symptoms. This shows that some people are sensitized but never have allergic symptoms, so that the presence of a positive skin test does not mean that person must have an allergy, but just that they have the potential to develop one. People with positive skin tests are more likely to develop allergies in the future than those with no positive tests.

The reverse situation is sometimes seen as well, where someone obviously has hayfever, yet the skin tests are negative to grass pollen. The diagnosis of hayfever can be proved in this type of case by a challenge or provocation test. There is no full explanation for this, except to say that skin testing exploits the skin as a test-organ and this assumes that what happens in the skin of your forearm accurately mirrors what happens in the organ affected by allergic reactions during natural exposure. This is not always so. Of course there are other reasons for negative tests. Preparing the extracts for tests is difficult, so the extract may be ineffective or at too low a concentration, or may simply have deteriorated because of storage. A final note of caution. Very occasionally skin tests can lead to a severe reaction, so they must always be done by an experienced doctor. This is terribly rare. Skin tests are safe in the very young, and in people with eczema, provided it is not so severe as to make testing difficult.

Intradermal tests

When the scratch skin tests are negative, yet there is a strong suspicion that a particular substance is causing the allergy, some allergists use intradermal tests. (If a skin test is positive, then there is no point in proceeding to an intradermal test.) A very low dose of the allergen is injected into the skin with a needle and syringe, and a positive reaction may be seen where the scratch or prick test was negative. This sort of test can occasionally provoke a serious reaction and must only be done by an expert. There is some evidence that intradermal tests can detect some types of allergy caused by other types of antibody than IgE. Often many injections at different concentrations are needed. The injections are not entirely painless, particularly when reactions are provoked. The tests can be time-consuming, and the results may not alter treatment very much anyway.

Patch tests

Patch tests are special skin tests which are used in the diagnosis of eczema due to allergy. As we said in Chapter 3, this type of allergy is due to T lymphocytes and not IgE. The reactions are therefore delayed, and so allergic contact eczema is a chronic condition rather than occurring in the acute attacks typical of other allergies. Patch tests are done by applying the suspected allergens to the skin under watertight dressings. No pricking with needles is necessary, the allergen simply seeps through the skin during the prolonged contact, just like the natural contact suspected of provoking the allergy in the first place. The skin of the back is normally used. The dressings are removed two to four days later, and if the allergen causing the eczema was included in one of the patches, it will have produced an eczematous rash. Although easy in principle, these tests should be done by an expert as getting the dose of allergen under each patch may be crucial. If there is no clue as to what the allergen might be in a particular case, then a battery of the common causes of allergic eczema can be used in patch tests. These are nickel (in jewellery), cobalt, chromates and various other industrial agents, such as formaldehyde and epoxy resins. Finally, ointments and creams containing various agents may themselves be responsible.

More complicated tests

There are more complicated tests for allergy than the skin tests we have just mentioned. It is easy to assume that because they are done in laboratories, they are more accurate in the diagnosis of allergy. This is quite mistaken, for they are very often less accurate or even misleading. There is no substitute for a detailed study of your symptoms perhaps backed up by simple skin tests.

Blood tests

Blood tests are usually unnecessary for allergy testing. However, the amount of IgE antibody in the blood can be measured, and its level may be increased in up to two thirds of people with allergies. But a high level of IgE can be caused by various other non-allergic conditions, such as infestation with intestinal parasites which we mentioned earlier, so measurement of IgE is not very useful, particularly as it does not tell you what the allergy is due to.

The RAST test

The RAST (radio-allergo-sorbent test) measures the tiny amount of IgE antibody present in the blood that is directed towards a particular allergen. This is obviously much more useful than just measuring the total IgE. As the way the RAST test is done is ingenious, it is worth describing briefly. The suspect allergen, say grass pollen, is stuck down on to paper discs. Blood from the person suspected of having hayfever due to grass pollen allergy is then added. If it contains any IgE against the pollen extract it will stick on. Finally, a special antibody directed against IgE is added. If any IgE has stuck on to the allergen, then the anti-IgE will bind on to it. This anti-IgE antibody is attached to a radio isotope label, so even when very tiny amounts become attached they can be detected in a sensitive radioactivity counter to give a positive test (Fig. 7). So the RAST can pick up very tiny amounts of IgE antibody directed against many common allergens, for example to pollens, moulds, dust mites and foods.

Does the RAST have any advantages over skin tests? Usually not. Skin tests are extremely sensitive, slightly more so than the RAST. If the RAST is positive, the skin test will always be positive, but if the skin test is positive then the RAST will be positive in only 90 per cent of cases. The RAST is useful where the skin

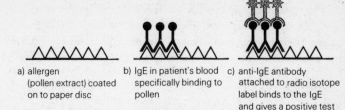

a) allergen (pollen extract) coated on to paper disc

b) IgE in patient's blood specifically binding to pollen

c) anti-IgE antibody attached to radio isotope label binds to the IgE and gives a positive test

Fig. 7.   The RAST test.

test results are not clear-cut or disagree with the suspected allergens, as here a RAST can settle the issue. Also the RAST can be done when skin tests cannot, for example in children who have severe eczema, or those with a positive reaction to the negative control on the skin test. Skin tests are quick, cheap and reliable. RAST is expensive and you have to wait for the result. Also the RAST is not helpful when it comes to food allergy.

Provocation tests

These are used when skin tests or RAST have failed to help in diagnosis or the diagnosis is difficult for other reasons. They are only very rarely needed. The principle is quite simple. Instead of applying the allergen to the skin as in a skin test, it is applied directly to the organ suffering the symptoms and so is intended to provoke symptoms in just the same way as they would be provoked by natural exposure to the allergen in the environment.

HAYFEVER AND RHINITIS

A small quantity of, say, pollen extract is sprayed up the nose (after the person has breathed in to prevent it getting into the lungs) to see if symptoms of hayfever are produced. A further refinement is to measure the nasal resistance to airflow before and after allergen, in addition to noting symptoms of sneezing, itching, watery discharge and blocking. The nasal resistance will increase with a positive test.

ASTHMA

The same principle applies, but it is only very rarely necessary to do this test. The suspected allergen is inhaled and the degree of wheezing is then measured. This test can trigger a major asthma attack and so must only be done in hospital by experts.

FOOD ALLERGY

This whole topic is generally more difficult than respiratory allergy, as the symptoms are often not clear-cut and skin tests are usually unhelpful. If a particular dietary substance is suspected of causing an allergy, a food challenge test may help. First that food must be totally eliminated from the diet for a period of time. Then the food is given, contained in a gelatine capsule or passed down a tube directly into the stomach so that it cannot be tasted. Any reaction is then observed. On another day the process is repeated, but with a totally non-allergic food. This is the dummy or placebo. Neither patient nor doctor should know which is given first and which is given second, so that psychological factors cannot interfere with the test. Even this degree of sophistication is not foolproof, as a sudden burst of the allergen given in the test is not the same as the continuous exposure to it that may occur naturally.

Other tests

Many other tests have been devised and advocated by some practitioners, but none are yet in regular use by the majority of allergy experts because so far there is no scientific evidence to justify their use. Some examples follow.

THE HISTAMINE RELEASE TEST

Some blood is taken from the allergic person and mixed with the suspect allergen. Blood contains a certain kind of white blood cell rather like the mast cells. When the correct allergen is added, the mediator histamine is released and measured. This is a complicated, expensive test and its main value is in research.

THE SUBLINGUAL TEST

Some substances are absorbed quickly from the mouth. The suspect allergen is put under the tongue and any reaction is noted. It is used by some practitioners to test for food allergies, but has not been clearly shown to be of any value in diagnosis.

THE CYTOTOXIC TEST

This has been popular in the USA for years for diagnosing food allergy. White blood cells taken from the patient are mixed with various food allergens. If the cells are damaged or killed by a particular allergen, this is a positive test. It has never gained general acceptance and there is nothing so far to suggest that it should.

The best test?

For the majority of allergies the skin test remains the best, the quickest and the cheapest test, and agrees with the more sophisticated challenge tests in about 80 per cent of cases. Skin tests are more sensitive than RAST, but RAST has its uses. A final word on skin tests. What if you have positive tests but no symptoms? It has been shown that you then have an increased risk (between four and ten times as great) of developing an allergy compared to someone with negative tests.

In this chapter we have looked at the spectrum of allergic diseases and the sort of tests doctors use to diagnose them. In the next part of the book we look at allergic diseases in detail, together with what you can do to get rid of them and what help you can get from your doctor.

PART TWO

Chapter Five

The Nose, Ears and Eyes

What is allergic rhinitis?

The first contact we have with the air we breathe is via the nose. The nose is designed to filter out rubbish and warm the air before it reaches the lungs. It has a moist corrugated lining, a bit like a radiator, so it is ideally suited to this purpose. But pollen grains, spores and dust are just the right size to land in the nose, so it is not surprising that the nose is a major black spot as far as allergy is concerned.

Allergic rhinitis just means an inflamed nose due to allergy. When an allergen lands in the nose, allergic inflammation of the moist mucous membrane lining is triggered and all the symptoms of rhinitis stem from this. People with allergic rhinitis also have a more sensitive nose than usual, and may get symptoms with changes in temperature and humidity and with fumes or smoke as well as contact with allergens.

Allergic rhinitis usually starts in childhood or early adolescence. It can be mild or severe, can happen in short, sharp, unexpected attacks, or can last all the year round.

What is hayfever?

This is just another word for seasonal allergic rhinitis. It is the commonest type of allergic rhinitis and as many as one in five people get it. In the UK the commonest cause is allergy to various grass pollens. In the USA ragweed pollen is the common cause, and in hot climates Bermuda grass. Doctors sometimes call hayfever 'seasonal pollenosis' which just means inflammation caused by pollen. Hayfever affects mainly the nose, but eyes, ears, throat, mouth and lung can also be involved. Hayfever has nothing to do with hay – it is caused by pollen. It has nothing to do with fever either, although victims may feel 'feverish'. The temperature is always normal.

What are the symptoms of allergic rhinitis?

There are three main symptoms: sneezing, watery discharge and blocked nose. Sneezing due to irritation of the nasal lining can happen in unpredictable outbursts, and is often the first sign of an attack. Irritating stuffiness of one or both nostrils due to swelling of the lining can lead on to complete blockage of the nose. This can come and go in a few hours or may last for days, and means you have to breathe through the mouth. The lining of the nose can produce an intense watery discharge, run like a tap and add to the discomfort. This is worse if your nose is completely blocked, as then you cannot sniff so your nose just drips. This misery punctuated by outbursts of sneezing can make normal life almost impossible.

The length and severity of an attack depend on the length and amount of exposure to the allergen. A brief encounter with a cat may mean only a sneezing spasm, but severe house dust mite allergy may mean a permanently blocked dripping nose all year round. But a mild case of house dust mite allergy may just have slight nasal stuffiness and a few sneezes first thing in the morning which quickly clear on getting up.

Other symptoms

Itching of the eyes, ears, mouth, palate and throat are quite common. During severe attacks the victim may feel generally ill, drowsy, irritable and unable to concentrate. Children get fractious, listless and sleep poorly. They often have mouth breathing, snore at night, have dripping noses which they rub continuously. They may sniff a lot and develop ear and sinus problems. Some cases of allergic rhinitis (about 10 per cent) have associated asthma and wheezing.

The eyes

Allergic conjunctivitis is often part of hayfever or other types of allergic rhinitis. The eye can behave very like the nose. Watering, itching and reddening, often with swelling of the surrounding eyelids, is common. The conjunctiva (the membrane covering the white of the eye) can swell up and have a bulging glassy look as well as becoming red and inflamed. The itching often makes rubbing of the eye irresistible, and this only makes the itching and swelling worse. The swelling can actually close the eye completely, and the inflammation can make it painful to look at bright lights. Sometimes allergic conjunctivitis occurs without rhinitis. For example, if you are allergic to hamsters and have just handled one and then you rub or touch your eye, you may trigger such an attack.

Complications of allergic rhinitis

These usually develop only in the more severe and chronic cases, particularly when symptoms persist throughout the year, with a troublesome almost permanently blocked nose.

Nasal polyps and loss of smell

Our sense of smell relies on special nerve endings in the nose. If the nasal lining is swollen and the nose is blocked, it is hardly surprising that loss of smell is quite common in rhinitis. Nasal polyps are thickenings of the nasal lining which grow into the nasal airway, dangling down like grapes and blocking the nose permanently. Your doctor will be able to see them quite easily on looking up your nose. Polyps tend to occur in older children and adults. They may provoke sinus trouble, and persistent infection in the nose.

The sinuses

These are air-filled cavities in the skull bone that are linked to the nose by quite narrow channels. If the nasal lining swells up, or if there are polyps, these channels can easily get blocked. This means that the sinuses, which normally produce small amounts of watery secretion, cannot drain properly. They can then get infected, produce thick yellow secretions and cause fever, headache and face pain. An acute sinusitis (that is, coming on suddenly) can be a most unpleasant illness requiring antibiotic treatment. Chronic long-standing sinusitis with persistent yellow discharge and headaches can add greatly to the misery of those with a chronic nose problem.

Can the ear be affected by allergy?

There is some uncertainty about this, and opinions vary. There is an air-filled cavity in the skull between the eardrum and the brain called the middle ear. Its function is to transmit the vibrations from the eardrum to the brain. It remains air-filled because there is a tube (the Eustachean tube) running from an opening at the back of the nose into the middle ear. This keeps it supplied with air. This tube is very narrow in little children and it can easily get blocked. If it blocks, the middle ear gradually fills up with fluid, the fluid becomes thicker and thicker, and deafness results as the thick glue-like stuff interferes with sound transmission. This is called 'serous otitis media', and leads on to 'glue ear'. Glue ear is the commonest cause of deafness in young children and may delay or prevent speech development. It is usually picked up by routine hearing tests at school clinics. Most are probably due to infections in the nose and throat such as tonsillitis, whereas others may possibly be due to allergic inflammation in the nose leading to blockage of the Eustachean tube. No one really knows. Anti-allergy medicines do not help the condition much, whereas antibiotics can in those cases where infection is important. Treatment by a small operation to restore air to the middle ear may be needed. Other cases clear up on their own. The operation is done by putting a tiny tube through the eardrum. If the tonsils and adenoids are greatly enlarged, they are often removed.

What are the main causes of allergic rhinitis?

The main causes of allergic rhinitis are the airborne allergens. The main ones are grass and tree pollen, house dust, the house dust mite and animals, including household pets. The importance of the others, like spores from fungi and moulds, is not clear yet.

How can allergic rhinitis be diagnosed?

The symptoms and the things that bring them on are so typical that there is usually no problem in diagnosis. If you or your doctor require confirmation, skin tests with extracts of the common airborne allergens will clinch the diagnosis. Very occasionally a skin test to pollen is negative in an obvious case of hayfever. No one knows why this is. Further confirmation can be achieved by a nasal challenge with pollen, but this is rarely necessary.

Can allergic rhinitis be confused with anything else?

The common cold is said to cause at least 60 per cent of all illnesses in the family. Most of us have about four colds per year. Colds are rare in babies under three months and are most common in the one-to-five year age bracket. After adolescence the number of colds we get tends to drop. They are caused by virus infections in the nose and throat. Colds produce symptoms which may be confused with allergic rhinitis, but there are some differences which make it quite easy to tell the two apart. First, we catch colds but allergies obviously are not infectious. An attack of allergic rhinitis can literally hit us out of the blue, but colds usually have a build-up over several hours or even a day. With a cold, sneezing and watery discharge tend to be less than with allergic rhinitis. Colds may give a temperature, sore throat, cough and make us feel generally unwell. These do not happen with allergic rhinitis. With colds, the eyes are not affected, and nasal discharge may become thick and yellow. Colds last between four and seven days. Allergic rhinitis is more variable, from an attack lasting a few minutes to permanent symptoms. The lining of the nostril is usually red during a cold but pale pink or even a greyish colour during allergic rhinitis. In children, as colds and rhinitis are both so common, confusion can occur and a 'permanent' cold with continuous sneezing and blocked nose may turn out to be allergic rhinitis. In any event, if you or your child develop a blocked nose that does not clear in a few days, go and see your doctor, as there are other causes as well.

Vasomotor rhinitis

This strangely named condition gives symptoms similar to allergic rhinitis but it does not seem to be allergic. The main symptom is a blocked nose which can shift from one nostril to the other and is often present all year round. It is uncommon in children (unlike allergic rhinitis) and usually starts in early adult life. There is no sneezing and eye trouble, and only a little watery discharge. The lining of the nostril is often red, rather as in a cold. Attacks are triggered by changes in temperature or humidity and smoky atmospheres rather than by allergens. Also, vasomotor rhinitis often does not respond as well to treatment as allergic rhinitis.

Treatment of allergic rhinitis

There are three lines of attack: (1) avoiding the allergen; (2) treatment with medicines; (3) desensitizing injections.

Avoiding the allergen

If the allergen can be avoided, the cause of the rhinitis is removed, allowing recovery. But avoidance is only possible for a few allergens, for example a food that is not a normal part of the diet, or an animal that is only rarely encountered. During the hayfever season, pollen is everywhere and cannot be avoided. The pollen count is published in the papers and represents the amount of pollen collected by the counter during the previous twenty-four hours. The pollen count varies widely from region to region. Generally the pollen count is lower indoors, so stay indoors as much as you can and avoid places where the pollen count is likely to be high, that is, where there is a lot of grass. Some people with intolerable hayfever find relief by having a holiday abroad somewhere away from pollen. If you are allergic to house dust and the house dust mite, then you can cut down your exposure by regular vacuum cleaning of the bedroom and by making sure it is well ventilated, cool and dry. Remove as many soft furnishings as you can, and even the carpet if possible. Finally, consider swapping to a foam rubber mattress and pillow. Dust mite allergy is less of a problem in hot countries, where people sleep in sparsely furnished, well ventilated rooms with the minimum of bedding. If you are an animal lover and have lots of pets and are allergic to them, then you have difficult decisions ahead. But if your child is strongly allergic to a pet, you really must seriously consider getting rid of it, perhaps settling for a goldfish instead. It is not good for children to have chronic allergic symptoms. They will miss school time and be unable to enjoy life to the full. If they also get asthma with their rhinitis, this is even more important. If contact with the pet continues, the allergy will continue and may even get worse. Finally, if moulds and spores are the problem, check the house for rising damp, dry rot and other fungal horrors. If you are successful in removing the cause of your own or your child's allergy and the symptoms disappear, remember that you are still probably allergic and will get symptoms again if re-exposed.

Treatment of allergic rhinitis with medicines

As pollen is so difficult, if not impossible, to avoid without going to extraordinary lengths, most people with troublesome rhinitis take medicines for it. Anti-allergy medicines do not cure allergy, they only suppress the symptoms. This means that they have to be taken continuously, as symptoms return if they are stopped. This can be a nuisance but not as big a nuisance as having allergic rhinitis. Treatment with medicines, if they are correctly taken, is nearly always successful except in the most severe cases.

Yet there are many people with rhinitis who suffer symptoms despite being on medicines, or who have abandoned treatment because it does not seem to work. All this is unnecessary. There is now a wide selection of different effective medical treatment and there should be something to suit everybody.

Two things may spoil treatment. First, sufferers give up the treatment too quickly because it does not seem to be working. Give it a chance. Some medicines need time to build up an effect. If it really does not seem to be working, don't give up, go back and tell the doctor. There is probably something more effective you can try. Everybody is different, so a certain amount of trial and error is inevitable to get successful control of symptoms. Second, it is easy for a doctor to underestimate the devastating misery of bad allergic rhinitis, and so to under-treat it. Now that we have greatly improved stronger medicines, this is unnecessary. Good control with virtually no side effects should be the rule rather than the exception for allergic rhinitis.

Another point about medicines. It does not matter what the allergen is that is causing your rhinitis – the treatment is identical regardless of the cause.

Antihistamines

These are often very effective, particularly in mild cases. They reduce itching, dry up secretions and reduce some of the swelling of both nose and eyes. Antihistamines are usually taken as tablets by mouth, but sprays and drops for the nose are available. Generally they work better for seasonal rhinitis (hayfever) than for perennial rhinitis. The disadvantages are that if taken by mouth they may take a day or two to reach their full effect. Those that are most used are Piriton, Benadryl, Anthisan, Fabahistin and Phenergan. The main problem is that they are all inclined to cause drowsiness, which can interfere with school or work, driving or operating machinery. They also have an additive effect with alcohol. Some are not suitable for children. The other side effects which are less common are dry mouth, blurred vision and dizziness. There are two new antihistamines which are proving more successful, as they do not produce drowsiness. Many people find them acceptable whereas the older antihistamines were not. These are Triludan and Hismanal. Hismanal has the advantage that you only have to take it once daily. These two new drugs should not be taken during pregnancy. If you are trying to get pregnant, do not take them. Finally, remember that an antihistamine tablet will not bring instant relief. A day or two may be required for the full effect, so persevere and give them a chance.

Decongestants

These are usually nose drops, and are very popular because they immediately and effectively shrink down the swollen lining of the nose, with instant relief from blocking and stuffiness. But the effects are shortlived, and the dose has to be repeated frequently to maintain the effect. If they are used too frequently (more than four times daily) or for more than a few days (up to two weeks), there is often a rebound effect with much worse congestion when they are stopped. Also, the more you use them the less effective they become. If used for a long time they will damage the lining of the nose, so they cannot be generally recommended. They must be used, if at all, with care and only for a short time. They are useful to get rid of mild and infrequent symptoms, or to relieve congestion temporarily before an important occasion like a social event or an exam. They may also be useful in someone with bad rhinitis and a completely blocked nose who is starting on other treatment. By unblocking the nose temporarily, other sprays and drops can penetrate the nose and start to do their work. Some nose drops, such as Otrivine-Antistin, contain a mixture of a decongestant and an antihistamine. Also very popular but not generally to be recommended are tablets containing a mixture of a decongestant such as pseudo-ephedrine and an antihistamine. Examples are Actifed and Dimotapp. They are popular because they bring instant relief, but they may have side effects. There are now more modern and effective medicines.

SODIUM CROMOGLYCATE (RYNACROM/OPTICROM)

The first of these is sodium cromoglycate, which works by blocking the allergic reaction. It comes as a spray, as drops or powder for the nose, and as drops for the eyes. It does not give instant relief, but works by preventing the attacks from occurring at all, or at least by reducing their severity when they do occur. This protection against attacks or prophylaxis only works if the medication is taken regularly as prescribed even when there are no symptoms. It will not stop symptoms once an attack has started. Many people do not realize this and so discard prophylactic-type medicines before they have a chance to be effective. Sodium cromoglycate is useful for mild and moderate allergic rhinitis and conjunctivitis. It is extremely safe and has no important side effects at all. This safety makes it ideal for children.

STEROID AEROSOLS AND DROPS

First, what are steroids? Steroids are very powerful anti-inflammatory drugs and are used to treat many different sorts of diseases. They are in fact a strong version of a hormone called cortisol which we all make in our adrenal glands (part of our endocrine gland system) and which is essential to health. The steroid drugs are all related to cortisol and are more correctly called cortico-steroids. Because of their strong anti-inflammatory action, the steroid sprays and drops are very effective against allergic rhinitis by reducing secretion of mucus and swelling of the nasal lining. But, again, they do not give instant relief. Their action is prophylactic, preventing attacks in the first place, so that they must be used on a regular basis to be effective – usually twice a day. It may take as long as two weeks for the maximum benefits to build up. They are used in moderate and severe cases of rhinitis. Examples are Beconase (an aerosol), Betnesol (drops), Syntaris (a spray) and Dexa-Rhinaspray. They are probably all equally effective, but if the nose is completely blocked, drops may be better than sprays. Sprays and aerosols may not penetrate, whereas drops may. But drops need to be taken correctly. If you just tip your head back and squirt drops into your nose, they will run straight down your throat and make you cough. The way to do it is to lie face down on a bed and dangle your head over the edge. Then squirt the drops in and stay in that position for a few minutes so that the drops linger in your nose, seep through the nasal lining and really do their stuff.

Steroids have a bad name for side effects. What are the side effects of these drops and sprays? Many careful studies have shown that even after years of use there is no permanent damage to the lining of the nose. Nor do they get absorbed into the blood stream in sufficient amounts to give any of the side effects that taking steroids by mouth can. Burning and stinging of the nose and sneezing may occur. A few people get minor nose bleeds because of drying and crusting of the nasal lining due to the steroids. If you get a side effect don't give up, a different steroid may suit you better. Finally, steroid sprays and drops will shrink up nasal polyps.

STEROID DRUGS TAKEN BY MOUTH OR INJECTION

Some people with severe allergic rhinitis still get disabling symptoms despite using all the medicines we have mentioned so far. For these very severe cases that cannot be controlled any other way, some doctors will prescribe steroid tablets. A commonly used one is prednisolone. Steroid tablets are nearly always effective in controlling severe cases, but doctors are often reluctant to prescribe them because of the danger of side effects. But side effects are minimal provided steroids are taken for only a week or two at a time, so their use in severe cases may be justified, particularly if important events like exams are in jeopardy. Steroids can also be injected. Depo-Medrone and Kenalog are depot-steroid preparations, that is, after injection, they are slowly released into the blood stream over about three weeks. Tablets are probably preferable to these injections, as the dose can be tailored to the symptoms on a day-to-day basis. Again, for the severe hayfever sufferer who knows that he is usually incapacitated during the first two weeks of June, it may be wise to start steroids a day or two before expected symptoms rather than letting things get out of hand first. Steroid tablets are sometimes useful for chronic severe cases of perennial rhinitis, where the nose has become permanently blocked. A short course of tablets may open the nose up so that sprays and drops can then be used effectively.

SURGERY AND RHINITIS

Sometimes, in longstanding severe allergic rhinitis, the nasal lining becomes greatly thickened, the sinuses become blocked and infected or nasal polyps develop. These changes may not respond to any of the above treatments and surgery may be the only solution. Operations can be done to remove the thickened nasal lining to improve the airway, to remove nasal polyps and to drain blocked sinuses. These operations are usually effective in removing troublesome symptoms but they do not cure the underlying allergic process. This means that polyps and sinus trouble can recur and that further surgery may be needed from time to time.

TREATMENT FOR THE EYES

Sodium cromoglycate (Opticrom) is often effective in controlling eye symptoms. Decongestant-antihistamine drops (Otrivine-Antistin) are also available. Steroid drops are rarely needed and must only be used under expert guidance. This is because if infection is present in the eye, it may be made much worse. Finally, oral steroids will improve eye symptoms.

SO WHICH TREATMENT SHOULD I TAKE?

For mild cases, the doctor will probably recommend sodium cromoglycate drops for the nose or the eyes, perhaps together with an antihistamine. Decongestant drops can be used sparingly for intermittent symptoms. Moderate cases will usually respond to an antihistamine together with a steroid spray or drops, and short courses of steroid tablets are reserved for very severe cases.

HOW TO TAKE TREATMENT

Common sense is the best guide. Remember that you are taking treatment to remove symptoms and therefore the treatment should be balanced against them. You know your symptoms best, so if you are expecting a severe attack of hayfever, try to start treatment a few days before – if you nip the attack in the bud it will be easier to control. If you know you are going to be exposed to an animal you are allergic to, say on a weekend trip, start some treatment before you go. You also know your child best, and you will be the best judge of when to start treatment. Always consult your doctor, follow his advice and take the medication as he directs. He has seen far more cases of allergic rhinitis than you have. Also discuss with him when to stop or reduce your medicines. Taking treatment regularly will give the best results. All treatments except decongestant drops take time to work. If the treatment does not work or if you are unhappy with it, go and discuss it with your doctor. There are plenty of alternatives which can be tried until one is found that suits you.

Desensitizing injections

WHAT IS DESENSITIZATION?

Desensitization, or immunotherapy as it is also called, is done by giving repeated doses of allergen extract by injection to the allergy sufferer. The idea is that somehow the immune system responds to this and the person as a result becomes desensitized, that is, loses the allergy altogether. The great attraction of this approach is that, if it works, it offers an actual cure for the allergy whereas drug treatment just damps down or suppresses the symptoms. But, to work, you have to identify the right allergen and then use injections of the correct allergen extract. With drug treatment it does not matter what the allergen is, the treatment works for all. Getting the allergen right can be tricky, particularly if a person has multiple allergies. This may account for some of the failures of desensitization.

The whole topic of desensitization, like so much else in the allergy field, arouses much argument. Some say it is an important solution to many sorts of allergy and should be used far more, others say it is useless or even dangerous and should be abandoned once and for all. As usual, there are no easy solutions, so now we will have to have a look at the evidence and try to reach a balanced conclusion about its value. But first of all, the technical details.

HOW IS IT DONE?

Firstly, skin testing is done to identify the allergen or allergens causing the symptoms. In some specialized centres, particularly in the USA, challenge tests (see Chapter 4) are also used to identify the culprit allergens, as some say they are more accurate in difficult cases.

Then the appropriate extract is selected and a very small dose is injected under the skin, usually in the arm. As the weeks go by, the injections are repeated and the dose is increased until fairly large doses are being given. Less frequent doses may then be given every few weeks as a booster. There are many different types of extract and dosage schedule for different allergens. A typical example is desensitization to grass pollen to prevent hayfever. Here, weekly injections are usually started in January and continue for three or four months, so that desensitization is completed before the start of the hayfever season.

One problem with desensitization is that it has been very difficult to standardize the extracts, so that the doses, intervals between injections and length of the course are all rather arbitrary. Trials on purified allergen vaccines and chemically altered extracts – 'allergoids', which may cause fewer side effects are under way, but there are no clear results yet.

DOES IT WORK?

The short answer is yes, but only in some cases. There is no doubt that some cases of hayfever and allergy to insect stings can be improved. It is probable that some cases of house dust mite allergy can also be improved. There are occasional reports of the odd dramatic improvement following desensitization to other allergens. The trouble is that it is not possible to know in advance who will benefit and who will not. There is no way of predicting.

DESENSITIZATION FOR HAYFEVER

In 1911, desensitization was done for the first time with boiled grass extract and was reported to have improved hayfever symptoms. A careful study done in the early 1950s showed that desensitization to grass pollen led to improvement in hayfever symptoms in almost 80 per cent of the cases, whereas dummy 'placebo' injections improved 30 per cent. This study showed a clear benefit with the active injections, yet raises the problem of the placebo effect where people get better anyway without the active treatment. This placebo effect can crop up in studies done on allergy treatment and makes it difficult to be sure that the treatment really does work. Studies done in the USA on ragweed pollen desensitization show that it works particularly in children.

Desensitization to just one type of pollen works better than desensitization to several. 'Cocktails' of several extracts do not seem to be as effective. This may be because smaller doses of each individual extract have to be given, because of side effects.

HOUSE DUST MITE DESENSITIZATION

Perennial allergic rhinitis due to dust mite allergy may be improved by desensitization. Some studies showed a benefit, others did not. Injections generally have to be given for at least a year. The conflicting results that are so often reported in all these studies may be partly due to the different schedules and types of extract used, the way the results are measured and the natural fluctuations in symptoms.

OTHER ALLERGENS AND DESENSITIZATION

Desensitization to animals can be done, but avoidance of the animal is better. This may not be possible where livelihood is concerned, as it is with vets, animal breeders and farmers. There is no clear answer as to how effective desensitization to animals is. Similarly, there is not much information on desensitization to moulds except that side effects are quite common. There are occasional reports of improvements following desensitization to food allergens but there is no substantial evidence of general usefulness yet. On the other hand, desensitization to insect sting venom is an effective and important treatment.

ASTHMA AND DESENSITIZATION

Again, results have been disappointing and conflicting. Asthma due to pollen or dust mite allergy, particularly in children, may be improved in some cases.

HOW DOES DESENSITIZATION WORK?

No one knows, but there are several theories. The first is that desensitization stimulates production of 'blocking antibody', which stops the allergen binding on to IgE antibody and activating mast cells. Second, that desensitization reduces the amount of IgE that is made. Neither of these theories is the whole story.

WHAT ARE THE DISADVANTAGES?

Firstly, desensitization is time-consuming and means many injections at regular intervals for months or even years. After each injection there is often some discomfort at the injection site, with itching or swelling. Occasionally there is a large reaction, and this is an indication that the next dose should be reduced. People have tried to get away from injections by putting vaccine directly into the nose. The problem here is that this too can provoke quite severe reactions. Another approach has been to give vaccines under the tongue, from where they are absorbed, or simply to swallow them. This should completely avoid side effects. Again, the evidence is in conflict, but generally this approach does not seem to work.

More severe reactions to the injections are fortunately rare but include attacks of asthma, urticaria or rhinitis following injections. Very rarely, an acute massive reaction (anaphylaxis) can follow, and this is potentially fatal. Deaths have been reported. This is why injections should always be given under medical supervision. The person who has received the injection should be observed for two hours after each injection to check that there is no reaction, and adrenaline, which is the antidote for a major reaction should be on hand. There is major concern at the moment as twenty-six patients, mostly young, have died in the UK since 1957 (five in the last eighteen months) from anaphylactic reactions to desensitizing injections. Because of this and doubts about whether desensitization is effective in the first place, it may be used far less in the future.

SO WHAT IS THE ROLE OF DESENSITIZATION?

In the USA and Europe, desensitization is popular despite all its disadvantages and is used a lot, particularly for grass and ragweed allergy. In the UK it is not used nearly so much because medical treatment is nearly always effective. Very few people should need to be desensitized. These are people with insect-sting allergy, and those with terrible hayfever who cannot take the medicines for one reason or another. Should people with very bad hayfever that cannot be controlled with steroid sprays and anti-histamines be desensitized? As the hayfever season usually lasts just a few weeks, it is probably better to use a short course of steroid tablets which will give a sure result rather than chance the uncertainties of desensitization.

Chapter Six

The Lungs – Asthma

Asthma is probably the commonest potentially serious disorder where allergy can play an important part. About one person in twenty will have asthma at some stage. Until quite recently asthma was an object of dread, conjuring up visions of feeble wheezy children who had to attend special schools. Luckily this negative view can be safely dropped, as the revolution in the treatment of asthma over the last twenty years means that the vast majority of asthmatics can now lead a normal life free of symptoms. Only an unlucky few with very severe asthma that does not respond so well to treatment are likely to be disabled with breathlessness.

What is asthma?

Asthma is the result of sudden widespread narrowing of the airways (the bronchi) in the lungs. The airways or bronchi are the branching system of tubes that carry air down from the mouth and into the lungs. Normally when the bronchi are wide open we are unaware of our breathing, as so little effort is needed to move air from the outside through the bronchi and down into the airsacs (alveoli) in the lung, where oxygen is taken up from the air into the blood stream. When the bronchi are narrowed there is a resistance to airflow in and out of the lung, much more work in breathing has to be done to overcome this resistance, and we feel breathless. This is what happens in a typical asthma attack. The key feature about asthma is that the airway narrowing is temporary and reversible. Either the narrowed airways relax and open up of their own accord and the asthma attack stops, or they relax when medication for asthma is taken. Why do the bronchi become narrowed? People with asthma all have one thing in common: their bronchi are hyper-reactive or 'twitchy', and have this tendency to go into spasm and narrow as a result of stimulation by a large number of different factors (allergy included), whereas a normal person's bronchi do not have this response. It is this increased 'twitchiness' of the bronchi in asthmatics that sets the scene for the asthma attack.

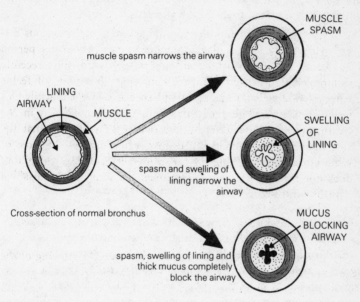

Fig. 8. Muscle spasm, swelling of the bronchial tube lining, and thick mucus narrow and block the bronchi in asthma.

The triggering of an asthma attack

Whatever it is that triggers or irritates the twitchy bronchi of an asthmatic into having an asthma attack, the bronchi become narrowed by three things (Fig. 8).

First, the muscle which lines the bronchi contracts or goes into spasm, and this tightening of the muscle narrows the airway. People who have had asthma for a long time have more muscle in their bronchi than normal – a bit like a weightlifter having big biceps. Second, the mucous membrane lining of the bronchi becomes inflamed and thickened. This produces further narrowing. Third, this lining pours out sticky mucus secretions, which cannot be cleared by coughing as they are thick and rubbery. This mucus further narrows or even blocks the airways altogether. All these effects can be produced, for example, by the mediators of allergic inflammation which are released from mast cells in the bronchial lining when they are triggered by allergens.

What are the symptoms of asthma?

The main symptom of asthma is breathlessness, which is caused by the narrowing of the bronchi. Breathlessness can be mild or very severe depending on the intensity of the attack. Breathlessness is usually accompanied by musical wheezing or whistling noises. These are produced by vibrations set up in the narrowed bronchi when air is forced down them, just like the vibration of a reed in a musical instrument. Asthma attacks can come on suddenly over just a minute or two, or can build up gradually over days or even weeks, and can last from just an hour or two, to weeks or even months. Some people have asthma in clear-cut attacks and are completely well otherwise, but others are wheezy or breathless to a greater or lesser extent all the time. As well as breathlessness and wheeze, asthmatics may feel uncomfortable as they breathe, with chest tightness and even chest pain during severe attacks. This is partly because the chest tends to swell up in asthma, as it is easier to get air in than to push air out when the bronchi are greatly narrowed, so the lungs tend to inflate to an uncomfortable extent. Normally we breathe quietly with our lungs half empty. Try breathing in as far as you can to the very top of your lungs and then try and breathe in a normal fashion but with your lungs full. It is very uncomfortable and you will quickly become tired. This is what a severe asthmatic has to put up with. Extremely severe attacks can lead to exhaustion from the sheer effort of breathing. In a bad attack, breathing is rapid, a lot of muscular work is required to breathe and the skin between the ribs and around the neck may be sucked in while breathing in because of the high pressures needed to get air in and out of the lungs, against the blocked airways.

Coughing is very often a major symptom too. Sometimes the cough is worse than the breathlessness, and can be particularly bad at night. The cough can be dry or wet with phlegm production. The phlegm may be white, grey or yellow. If it is yellow this may mean that infection is present, but not always. Generally speaking, asthma is very often worse at night and early in the morning. People with chronic asthma often find that their breathing is worst when they wake in the morning. Sometimes asthmatics wake in the middle of the night because they are so breathless. This is a reliable indication that the asthma is severe and needs an increase in treatment. Some people get asthma only at certain times of the year. This seasonal variation in asthma is a sign that it is due to an allergy.

How is asthma diagnosed?

From what we have just said, the diagnosis is very often obvious when someone is having bouts of breathlessness with wheeze and cough. The hallmarks of asthma are first, the spasmodic nature of the attacks, triggered by a wide range of factors, and second, the underlying bronchial hyper-reactivity or twitchiness with inflammation of the bronchi during the attacks.

Even so, the diagnosis is surprisingly often missed. A recent survey suggested that perhaps as many as 50 per cent of asthma cases are never diagnosed, but are mis-labelled as wheezy bronchitis, chronic bronchitis, chronic colds, chronic cough and so on. This is particularly true of children. It is important to make the diagnosis because now, as the treatment is so good, the symptoms can be removed in the majority of cases for most of the time. It is also important to diagnose asthma early because quick control minimizes suffering and disability. In some cases, failure to diagnose it is a disaster, as asthma is potentially fatal.

To make the diagnosis, if it is not obvious already, all that has to be done is to show that the degree of narrowing of the airways is variable. The airway narrowing can be measured with a simple gadget called a peak-flow meter. It measures how fast you can breathe out. If airways are narrow, the speed at which you can breathe out is greatly reduced and the meter shows a low reading. To get a reading you puff as hard as you can into the meter. Normal readings range from about 350–600 litres per minute, and the normal value for you depends on your age, sex and height. In a bad attack, this falls to around 100 litres per minute.

In someone with asthma, the readings vary quite a lot during the day. For example they are often at their lowest early in the morning. If there is doubt about the diagnosis, peak flow readings taken several times a day may show this variability and clinch the diagnosis. The peak flow readings will also give you and the doctor some idea of the severity of your asthma, so he may ask you to record readings you make yourself at home on a chart using a small portable meter.

What other tests are useful or necessary?

It is fairly routine to have a chest X-ray if you have a chest complaint like asthma. This is usually normal in asthma. In severe cases it may show minor enlargement of the lungs, due to the inflation problem we mentioned earlier. Skin tests to identify sensitivity to common allergens may be helpful in some cases.

What are the complications of asthma?

Sometimes part of a lung may collapse because the bronchi feeding it are completely blocked with mucus. Occasionally the asthmatic lung leaks some air outside its lining into the gap between the lung itself and the chest wall (ribs, etc.). This means the lung gets smaller and quite a lot of air can accumulate between the lung and the chest wall. This adds to the breathlessness and may give chest pain too. It is called a 'pneumothorax' (air in the chest).

Is all asthma due to allergy?

The answer is almost certainly no. Many other factors are responsible for asthma as well as allergy, and we will consider these in a moment. But first we must mention a distinction that doctors sometimes make when considering asthma. They often talk about 'extrinsic' and 'intrinsic' asthma. These two types of asthma behave differently, so it is worth going into some detail. Extrinsic asthma is asthma provoked by some obvious external agent, usually an allergen. When someone inhales an allergen to which he is sensitive, it lands on the lining of the bronchi and triggers the allergic response leading to narrowing of the airways, and so to asthma. Most cases of asthma that start in childhood are extrinsic or allergic in nature, and about 80 per cent of all asthmatics under thirty years of age have this type. Extrinsic asthma tends to run in families and to be associated with exzema and hayfever. Skin tests to allergens are usually positive, and response to treatment is usually excellent. It is often easy to identify the allergens causing the attack, as attacks start soon after exposure. For example, in people with pollen allergy, wheezing may start a few minutes after walking through a field during the grass-pollen season, or in someone allergic to cats, within moments of going into a room where a cat has been.

With intrinsic asthma there is nothing to suggest that allergy plays a part. There is no relation between attacks and exposure to possible allergens, and allergy skin tests are negative. Attacks are often triggered by colds or other chest infections. There is also an association with nasal polyps and asthmatic reactions to aspirin. Less than 10 per cent of children with asthma have this type (i.e. intrinsic), which is commoner in older age groups. Sixty per cent of asthmatics over thirty years of age have the intrinsic type, and about 80 per cent of those who get their first attack of asthma over the age of sixty. Treatment is usually less effective in this type of asthma.

To return to allergy, quite a lot of asthma has an allergic basis and is triggered by allergic reactions. As you get older, allergy plays less of a part, but even so it is estimated that allergy is an important factor in 50–70 per cent of adult asthmatics.

What are the allergens that cause asthma?

The allergens that cause seasonal asthma (very much like seasonal rhinitis, i.e. hayfever) are the pollens and possibly the mould spores which we discussed in the previous chapter. Tree pollen allergy may lead to asthma in the spring, grass pollen to summer attacks, and weed pollen allergy to attacks in late summer or early autumn. Asthma related to mould-spore allergy may crop up at any time or may be present all year round, but there is a peak in the autumn. Overall, acute (that is sudden and severe) asthma attacks are most frequent in the summer and again in the autumn, underlining the importance of allergy.

The most common cause of allergic asthma lasting throughout the year is the house dust mite. Pets present in the home throughout the year may also provoke continuous asthma in the allergic. Intermittent attacks of asthma not related to the seasons are often due to exposure to allergens that are not normally present. Animals or moulds are quite often responsible and sometimes the dust mite too. Common examples are when you visit a friend's house where there are pets, or stay at a relative's for the weekend where the bedroom may be damp, encouraging mould, or be full of old bedding and carpets harbouring armies of house dust mites. Among animals, cats seem to be a particular problem as far as allergic asthma is concerned. This may be because one of the major cat allergens is in the saliva and cats are always licking their coats, providing an ideal way of spreading it around. Obviously the degree and length of time of exposure determine whether the asthma attack is sudden, persistent, mild or severe.

Items of food can provoke allergic asthma attacks, but these are less common than attacks due to airborne allergens. Frequently, with food allergy, the asthma attack is accompanied by sudden itchy skin rashes, vomiting or diarrhoea. As with other allergens, people can be allergic to one or several foods. Food allergy, as we will describe later, is often much more difficult to sort out than the other allergies. Some food allergies provoke immediate asthmatic reactions within thirty minutes, and these are obvious. Common examples are allergy to fish, shell fish, nuts, fruit and tartrazine (an orange dye used to colour some processed foods and drinks). Allergy to foods eaten all the time may provoke chronic asthma, due to so-called 'late reactions' which do not come on suddenly but build up gradually and are generally more difficult to identify. The common examples here are allergy to egg, milk, flour and cereals. Some people get asthma following various alcoholic drinks. This is not due to the alcohol itself but to other substances in these drinks.

Which are the commonest causes of allergic asthma? A recent survey in a group of people with allergic asthma showed that 80 per cent had positive skin tests to house dust and the house dust mite, 60 per cent to various pollens, 40 per cent to cats, dogs, etc., 25 per cent to spores of fungi and moulds, and 15 per cent to various foods. But remember that a fair number of people with no allergic symptoms whatsoever have positive tests to all these things, so skin tests are a rough guide only.

What else triggers off asthma besides allergy?

Two phases are important in producing an asthmatic attack. First, as we have already said, the bronchi have to be hyper-reactive or 'twitchy'. This is what 'being an asthmatic' is. It means you are prone to getting attacks. This original twitchiness may be due to a number of different things. It has not yet been sorted out.

Second, a stimulus is required to trigger the twitchy bronchi into an actual asthma attack. We have already mentioned the allergens which can do this, now we will list the other things that trigger attacks.

INFECTIONS AND ASTHMA

Another important trigger of asthma attacks is infection. Asthmatics often find that their attacks are set off by colds, sore throats or flu. This may be because infection causes further damage to the already sensitive bronchial lining and so sparks an attack. Most of these infections are due to viruses, against which antibiotics are ineffective.

EXERCISE

Up to 80 per cent of all asthmatics sometimes get wheezy and breathless about five minutes after starting vigorous exercise. In fact some asthmatics only get attacks during exercise. This is more marked in cold dry weather. Exercise-induced asthma usually lasts about half an hour, and if exercise is continued through the attack, it may gradually wear off. Generally, running is more likely to bring it on than cycling, and cycling more so than swimming. A child or young adult who gets excessively breathless during exercise may in fact have exercise-induced asthma. This sort of asthma is thought to be due to cooling and drying of the bronchial lining. The rapid increase in breathing that occurs when exercise starts means that air reaches the lungs without having time to warm up. This leads to mast cells releasing their mediators and triggering an attack. Once identified, treatment is usually effective. Sodium cromoglycate (Intal) or salbutamol (Ventolin) taken by aerosol puffer a few minutes before exercise starts will block the attack.

IRRITANTS IN THE AIR

Fumes, cigarette or other smoke, and atmospheric pollution due to gases such as sulphur dioxide can trigger asthma, as can cold dry air or sudden changes in temperature. These things provoke asthma by irritating the bronchial lining directly rather than by allergy. Many asthmatics find that they cannot cope with going into smoky pubs, or get severe attacks when they do painting and decorating.

Is asthma psychological?

A few doctors and patients still think that asthma is caused by stress or neurosis, and so is really 'all in the mind'. Most experts now think it unlikely that psychological factors like stress, anxiety, fatigue and emotional upsets actually cause asthma, as the tendency to have asthma attacks depends on a physical condition of the bronchi, namely hyper-reactivity or twitchiness. But it is equally clear that actual attacks can be triggered or made worse by psychological upsets of various kinds, including anxiety, stress and recent bereavement. Many asthmatics notice that their attacks are much worse when they are under stress.

Yet having a severe acute asthma attack is very frightening, as you feel you cannot breathe properly. It is quite natural to feel anxious and panicky. The same applies if you are having a long-drawn-out attack and cannot sleep for weeks on end. You are bound to be irritable, nervous, and emotionally labile. When the asthma is treated, the anxiety goes away as well. Clearly the relation between mind and body is complicated as far as asthma is concerned, and the cause-effect relation can work in both directions. The exact way that all this functions is not sorted out, but research is beginning to suggest interesting connections between our brains and our bronchi which would explain what we have just said. Certainly, the bronchi have a rich supply of nerves from the brain which have some control over the bronchial muscles.

Asthma related to work

Various special dusts and fumes present in the environment can cause asthma in some people. If these are dusts and fumes encountered at work, often from rather unusual substances, then the asthma is said to be occupational. The main point is that a person can develop hypersensitivity to a particular substance at work resulting in asthma. So there is a gap between starting the job where the fumes and dust are and starting to get asthma. This gap can be between a few weeks and several years. Some types of occupational asthma are more common in allergic people, some not. Some types have been shown to be due to development of definite allergy to the inhaled substances, but in others it remains unknown how the asthma is produced.

Not everyone who is exposed to these various things gets asthma as a result, just a few. The type of asthma that develops depends on the dose and length of exposure, but generally wheezing and breathlessness tend to get worse as the day goes by, and are worse as the week progresses. Symptoms often clear up when away from work, that is at weekends and on holidays. Sometimes it is obvious what is causing the asthma, since attacks start quickly after breathing in fumes or dust. At other times, particularly if the exposure is continuous, the cause may not be so obvious and a detailed inquiry into substances in the work place may be needed. Diagnosis is often helped by keeping peak flow meter readings during the week, both at work and on holiday when the readings usually improve. Very occasionally a provocation challenge test (see Chapter 4) is needed to prove that a suspect substance is causing the asthma. This will be done at a special hospital centre. The asthma itself is treated in the same way as other types, and exposure to the cause should be stopped. This may mean changing jobs. When exposure stops, the asthma usually gets better.

What causes occupational asthma?

Over 200 different substances have been identified and the list is likely to grow. First there are chemicals (isocyanates, acid anhydrides, epoxy resins, formaldehyde, etc.) used to make plastics, paints, adhesives and glues, wrappers and wall insulation. Various metals have been identified as causing asthma and include nickel, chromium, cobalt and platinum. People involved in processing or refining these metals may develop asthma, indeed up to 40 per cent of platinum refiners can develop such asthma. Various fumes such as chlorine, ozone, sulphur dioxide and nitrogen oxides may provoke asthma if inhaled in confined surroundings. Wood dust (particularly Western Red Cedar) and dust from grain and flour may cause asthma in sawmill workers, farmers, millers and bakers. Workers in electronics factories may develop asthma from the fumes of solder flux, which contains a resinous substance called colophony. Hairdressers may run into trouble from henna and persulphates which are used in hair bleach. Asthma can also be caused by humidifiers in air-conditioning systems that have become contaminated with germs. Finally, people who make antibiotics in the pharmaceutical industry or enzyme detergents may get asthma from inhaling the dust, and laboratory workers and animal breeders can develop asthma from rats, mice and even locusts!

Asthma and medicines

Several medicines can trigger asthma. Some asthmatics get attacks when they take aspirin. This aspirin sensitivity is not allergic in nature but is due to a direct effect of the drug on the body. Many other pain-killing and anti-inflammatory drugs can have similar effects in aspirin-sensitive asthmatics. Paracetamol is the least likely to cause trouble. Certain drugs called beta-blockers, which are used for some cases of high blood pressure, are best avoided in asthmatics as they often make the asthma worse. People who are allergic to some antibiotics may get asthma attacks if they inadvertently take them.

The final common pathway in asthma

We have seen the enormous range of things, including allergy, that can start an asthma attack. They all somehow or other trigger the twitchy asthmatic airway into an attack. Now we must turn our attention to treatment, and first to what you can do for yourself or your child.

General measures to improve your asthma

First of all, look after yourself properly. Do not let your general health deteriorate, and avoid doing things that are obviously harmful to the health. Try and keep fit. Regular exercise is a good idea. Do not let yourself become overweight. The more weight you have on board, the more work you have to do carrying it around, and the harder your lungs have to work. So go on a sensible diet if you need one.

Stop smoking. There are several reasons why you should. First, on general health grounds, you will avoid the increased risks of cancer, heart attacks and other diseases that smoking brings with it. Second, you have sensitive airways. If you smoke you may trigger attacks or become persistently very wheezy. Third, if you smoke for a long time you may well develop chronic bronchitis as well as your asthma, then you really will be in trouble.

If stress and anxiety seem to be important in triggering

attacks, try to avoid situations that upset you. You have to be the judge here, but people have changed to a less stressful job before now for the sake of their asthma. Try not to let yourself get depressed and run down. It is easy to get dispirited if you have unpleasant chronic symptoms, but far better not to if you can avoid it. Where stress and anxiety are unavoidable, some asthmatics find that this makes them hyperventilate (breathe too rapidly) and this in turn triggers an attack. Learning how to relax with slow breathing exercises may be useful. Take note of what you eat and drink, and be on the look out for things that make your asthma worse so that you can avoid them.

Consider joining the Asthma Society and Friends of the Asthma Research Council. They have over 100 branches around the country, organize meetings and activities and publish a journal three times a year.

Allergen avoidance

We have already mentioned that allergen avoidance is not always easy. If dust mites are the problem then clean up the bedroom, get rid of the carpets, change to a foam rubber mattress and pillow or put them in plastic bags. Vacuum regularly. These mite-reduction measures do help, but they can never completely abolish the mite. Holidays in hot climates with tiled floors and minimal bedding often greatly improve allergic asthma. It has been shown that when children with dust-mite allergic asthma live for several months in a special mite-free environment in hospital, the asthma clears up. Obviously such extreme measures are not possible for most of us.

During the pollen season, the pollen count can be kept low indoors by keeping windows and doors shut. Unfortunately, just the short trip to work or school and back may expose you to enough pollen to keep your hayfever going all day.

If a pet is creating the allergy, and medicines are failing to keep control, the only solution is to get rid of it and then thoroughly spring-clean the whole house. If living without a pet is impossible, try changing it, or if this is not possible at least keep it out of the house and certainly out of the bedroom as far as possible. If mould spores upset you, try and eliminate damp from your home. Does it have a damp-proof course? Put extractor fans in the kitchen and bathroom to prevent condensation.

Finally, avoid the irritants. Do not use paints, sprays, cleaning materials or solvents in a confined unventilated room. Do not frequent pubs or other smoky places if cigarette smoke triggers attacks. If cold weather is bad for you and you have to go out, take some medication fifteen minutes before you have to leave the house.

The medical treatment of asthma

The mainstay of asthma treatment is drugs and medicines. These do not cure the asthma but suppress or damp down the asthmatic reaction, so they have to be taken continuously. Treatment with medicines is likely to remain the mainstay in asthma unless some way of turning off the asthmatic tendency is discovered.

The aim of treatment with medicines is to gain complete control of symptoms by having wide open bronchi all the time. This means preventing as far as possible severe acute attacks and also abolishing chronic wheeze and breathlessness. Broadly, there are two types of asthma medicine: the first relieves the muscle spasm so the bronchi open up, the second reduces the inflammation in the airways and prevents attacks building up. The first are called bronchodilators because they dilate or open-up the bronchi.

BRONCHODILATORS

The most potent and most used are a family of drugs related to adrenaline (the old-fashioned but very effective anti-asthma drug which is also a hormone made in our own adrenal glands). They work like adrenaline and relax bronchial muscle but have far fewer side effects. They are extremely safe and they usually continue to work no matter how much you use them. They give almost instant relief, and the good effects on the breathing last for about four hours after each dose. There are several and there is not much to choose between them (Ventolin, Bricanyl, Berotec, Pulmadil, Alupent). The easiest way to take them is with an aerosol puffer. This is a pressurized canister that releases a cloud of the drug when you set if off by pressing it. Technique is important here: the trick is to inhale as much of the cloud of mist as possible. You breathe out, put the nozzle in the mouth, trigger the aerosol by pressing the aerosol canister against the plastic container, and breathe in at the same time so that you suck the mist deep into the lungs. It is usual to take two puffs at a time, and as it lasts for about four hours, four or more doses may be needed each day. Some asthmatics may take doses even more frequently, but this should only be under a doctor's direction. Some people find it difficult to use the aerosol and there are now various gadgets to help. An alternative is the Rotahaler, which delivers the drug as a dust to the lung when it is sucked out of the container. The Rotahaler is particularly handy for children and the very old. Finally, bronchodilators like Ventolin can be taken with a nebulizer. This is a plastic container which is loaded with a solution of the drug and is attached to an air compressor which blows air through the solution, turning it into a fine mist which is then inhaled through a nozzle or face mask for a few minutes. The advantage of the nebulizer is that no special co-ordination is needed. You just breathe in and out normally with the nozzle in your mouth, and large doses of bronchodilators can be given quickly. The nebulizer is the standard treatment now for sudden and severe attacks. All hospitals, many general practitioners and some people with severe prolonged asthma have nebulizers. But for most asthmatics they are unnecessary. There has been recent concern about nebulizers used at home, as there have been some deaths associated with their use. This may be because people with very bad asthma take huge amounts of bronchodilator with the nebulizer and neglect their other vital treatment. Undue reliance on them may be unwise; they must be used only under a doctor's direction, and if they do not improve a severe attack you must call a doctor or go to the hospital accident and emergency department without delay.

Bronchodilators are generally more effective when inhaled and delivered direct to the lungs rather than when taken as tablets or by injection. Tablets (and syrup for children) are preferred by a few people, particularly when asthma is troublesome at night. Slow release tablets of Ventolin or Bricanyl can be taken last thing at night and may prevent an attack waking you in the early hours. In hospitals, these drugs are sometimes given as an intravenous injection for serious attacks. People worry about side effects. Bronchodilators are by and large extremely safe, do not become less effective with continuous use and do not cause long-term damage. If you take too much, your heart beat may speed up and become forceful and you may develop shaking of the hands. Neither of these are harmful and they will wear off in an hour or two.

Another type of bronchodilator called Atrovent is given in an aerosol and is found useful by many people with asthma. It provides quick relief like Ventolin-type drugs but acts in a different way.

The third type of bronchodilator is aminophylline. This cannot be given as an aerosol and is available as tablets, suppositories or injections. It is a good bronchodilator but takes time to work, as it has to be absorbed from the stomach. Slow-release tablets (Phyllocontin, Uniphyllin, Nuelin SA, Slo-Phyllin, etc.) that work through the night can be useful for asthma that is a problem at night. Suppositories are not much used now as absorption is unpredictable. Aminophylline preparations have side effects. Sometimes it is necessary for the doctor to measure the amount in the blood to get the dose right. Some people get nausea and vomiting. Overdoses (accidental or intentional) are dangerous. If you take aminophylline and your asthma gets worse, DO NOT just take more tablets. See your doctor. If you go to hospital with a bad attack and you take aminophylline tablets, the doctor may want to give you an intravenous injection. Be sure to tell him you are on the tablets so that he can lower the dose or use a different drug.

SODIUM CROMOGLYCATE (INTAL)

This is an anti-allergic drug, as we have already mentioned. It can be taken as an aerosol or as an inhaled powder and is most useful for preventing mild allergic asthma, particularly in children. It also prevents asthma provoked by exercise. Not everybody responds to it. It is often used together with a bronchodilator aerosol.

It has virtually no side effects, although a very few people find that it makes them cough.

ANTIHISTAMINES

These are largely ineffective in asthma and are not recommended.

STEROIDS

As we have said in Chapter 5, these drugs are the most potent anti-inflammatory drugs we have, and part of the revolution in the treatment of asthma has been due to the use of aerosol steroids. They reduce spasm and inflammation in the asthmatic airways if used regularly. Aerosols are the ideal way to take steroids as they go straight to where the trouble is, the bronchi, and because very little ever gets absorbed into the blood stream the side effects seen with taking steroid tablets do not occur. Aerosols (Becotide, Pulmicort, Bextasol) are usually taken twice, three or four times a day. Rotahalers are available for people who cannot use aerosols. For people with severe asthma, high-dose aerosols are available (Becloforte, Pulmicort). Aerosol steroids do not give instant relief but build up their effect gradually over days or even weeks to reach their maximal effect in preventing asthma attacks, so they must be taken regularly whether you are wheezy or not. The odd puff is useless. They are very often given in conjunction with an aerosol bronchodilator like Ventolin, although some asthmatics find they gain complete control on a steroid aerosol alone. What are the side effects? A few patients develop a throat infection (thrush) due to a fungus called *Candida*. Others very occasionally develop a hoarse voice. These side effects can be cut down by rinsing and gargling with water immediately after using the aerosol, to wash out all the steroid that gets deposited in the mouth. Otherwise aerosol steroids are safe and can be used for years without any long-term side effects.

STEROID TABLETS

There was a time when people with severe asthma had to take steroid tablets on a long-term basis to control their symptoms. The side effects they developed gave steroids a bad name. Nowadays only a very few people with asthma should need long-term steroid tablets.

Steroid tablets are now reserved for when all else fails. They are nearly always very effective against severe asthma. They are usually used now in short sharp bursts, for severe sudden attacks that do not get better with inhaler aerosols, and for severe chronic asthma, to get it better so that aerosols then have a chance to work. Quite a high dose is often used (30–60 mg of prednisolone per day – 6–12 tablets) for one or two weeks, after which the dose can be quickly reduced and stopped. Courses like this can be repeated as necessary. They are quite safe and side effects are relatively few, the commoner ones being weight gain, ankle swelling, acne and a feeling of being bloated. If you have a stomach ulcer or indigestion, oral steroids are best avoided, although coated tablets that pass through the stomach unaltered are available.

If you are unlucky enough to have very severe asthma that does not respond to the treatment we have discussed so far and you have to take steroid tablets on a long-term basis, then you may be at risk from side effects. These include high blood pressure, diabetes, indigestion, weight gain, muscle weakness, weakening of the bones and easy bruising of the skin. Also steroids must not be stopped suddenly, as long-term steroids prevent the adrenal gland making the normal amounts of cortisol. All this sounds terrible, but remember that asthma can be fatal, and the disadvantages of treatment always have to be weighed against the disadvantages of the asthma.

SO WHAT MEDICINE SHOULD I TAKE?

For mild occasional asthma, your doctor may prescribe an aerosol bronchodilator like Ventolin. Benefit will last for a few hours. For more frequent and severe attacks, a regular bronchodilator like Ventolin with either sodium cromoglycate or, if this does not work, with a regular aerosol steroid will usually be the next step. If there are still problems, your doctor may add in tablets of slow-release aminophylline, or put you on the high-dose steroid aerosol. For very severe attacks you may need short courses of steroid tablets under your doctor's directions. If you have bad attacks at night, tablets of slow-release aminophylline or Ventolin taken at bed-time may help. Remember that several medicines can be taken together with good effect and that your doctor may also prescribe an antibiotic for a bad attack if it seems to have been triggered by a chest infection. Finally, if your asthma is getting worse despite treatment, go and see your doctor at once. If he or she is not available, go to your nearest accident and emergency (casualty) department.

Desensitization injections for asthma?

As we said earlier, these probably work in a few cases of asthma caused by pollen allergy, and possibly in some cases due to house dust mite allergy. But they are time-consuming and sometimes unpleasant to have, and the medicines we have just described are nearly always more convenient and effective.

How do I know how severe an asthma attack is?

Some people with severe asthma find it difficult to gauge how bad an attack is, particularly if it has built up gradually. This is because they do not feel as breathless as you might expect from the severity of narrowing in their airways (bronchi). If you have severe asthma, then you may find the peak flow meter very useful in helping you to decide how bad your asthma is, and whether it improves after you have taken your bronchodilators.

Signs that asthma is becoming severe and is out of control are when inhaler aerosols do not have their usual effect in giving quick relief and if you start waking at night with breathlessness and wheeze.

Signs that asthma has become very severe and may need treatment in hospital are: finding it very difficult to breathe and breathing rapidly, getting tired and exhausted with the effort of breathing, getting restless, anxious, confused or drowsy, having a peak flow meter reading of less than about 150 litres per minute, having a rapid pulse (over 110 beats per minute) and being so breathless that you cannot complete a sentence when talking. If any of these happen, get medical help quickly or go straight to hospital. Remember that people with severe asthma do not always have loud wheezes. The breathing can be remarkably quiet during very severe attacks.

How is a very severe attack best treated?

If you start to have a bad attack, take your bronchodilator. This can be repeated after a few minutes. Do not take extra aminophylline tablets. If your doctor has instructed you to start yourself on steroid tablets whenever you get a bad attack, do so. If you are not better quickly or just get worse, then call your doctor or go to hospital immediately.

What will my own doctor do?

If your doctor visits you at home, he or she may decide you need to go to hospital or may decide to treat you at home. An injection of steroids or aminophylline may be given, or you may start on steroid tablets or antibiotics. The doctor may have a nebulizer and give you a dose of bronchodilator with it, or you may be given oxygen.

What happens if I go to hospital?

When you arrive in the accident department the doctor will probably measure your breathing with the peak flow meter and then give you some bronchodilators in a nebulizer. You will probably be given some oxygen through a face mask. The doctor will then get a chest X-ray done and do some blood tests. If your asthma does not pick up quickly you may be started on steroid tablets or even be given some drugs intravenously. Some people get dehydrated with asthma, so you may be given some liquids intravenously as well. Finally, you will be given antibiotics if there is anything to suggest infection. Even though you may not have slept properly for nights, the doctor will not give you sleeping pills as this can be dangerous. Most people who need to go into hospital get better very quickly in a few days, and then can stay well for months. So do not hold off visiting the doctor if the asthma is bad. A quick stay in hospital will save you time and distress in the long run.

How serious is asthma? Can it be fatal?

Fortunately most asthmatics respond well to modern treatment and have minimal inconvenience or disability. But asthma must be treated with respect, as it is a potentially fatal condition. Despite all the major advances in treatment over the last twenty years, asthma still kills about 1,500 people annually in England and Wales. Although asthma does not kill as many people as cancer or heart attacks, the figure is still far too high.

Why do people die? Recent surveys highlight several reasons. Sometimes the diagnosis of asthma is missed altogether, so that the wrong treatment is given. This can happen with children who are labelled as having 'wheezy bronchitis' and are treated with antibiotics instead of bronchodilator drugs. Sometimes, fortunately very rarely, attacks come on so suddenly that there is not time to get to hospital for intensive treatment. At other times the severity of the attack is underestimated by the patient or the doctor, and not enough treatment is given (for example, courses of steroid tablets are probably not used enough). This is where a peak flow meter can be helpful in allowing you to measure the severity and adjust your treatment accordingly. You know your asthma best. The doctor and the peak flow meter can help greatly as well. It can be easy to underestimate asthma, so try to develop a 'feel' for when it is good and when it is bad. Take the medicines prescribed *regularly*, whether you are wheezy or not. Prevention is the name of the game in asthma. This will reduce the chance of a surprise bad attack. Do not suddenly stop treatment without a doctor's advice. Do not hold back on increasing treatment when things are getting bad (but do *not* increase the number of aminophylline tablets you take, remember that they can be poisonous if too many are taken). It is easier to put things right by taking stronger medicines earlier rather than later. Do not put up with disabling wheeze and breathlessness, take the medicines. They are safe and effective if taken in the correct manner. Do not take sleeping pills or sedatives during bad attacks. If in doubt or if you are worried or frightened, go and see your doctor or visit the hospital immediately. Do not be frightened to take a short course of steroid tablets. Generally, asthma is not the serious condition it once was, provided effective treatment is taken regularly. We now have good effective treatment provided it is used properly. Research will lead to new better treatments as well. The days when effective treatment was not available and many asthmatics were condemned to an uncertain life of invalidism should now be well and truly over.

Can asthma permanently damage the lungs?

Obviously during an asthma attack the lungs are abnormal, as the narrowed bronchi prevent adequate movement of air in and out of the lungs and the work of breathing is increased. Between attacks the lungs are usually completely normal and no permanent damage is done. Only in very severe long-standing asthma, when the bronchial tubes are permanently very narrow, do the lungs become damaged. Some doctors think that this damage can be minimized if asthma is very well controlled with treatment to keep the bronchi as open as possible. This means taking enough regular treatment to keep as free from wheeze and breathlessness as possible.

Asthma and chronic bronchitis

These two conditions are often confused with each other. The symptoms of chronic bronchitis are cough, usually with sputum (phlegm), breathlessness and wheeze. The symptoms come on gradually over years and do not respond very well to treatment. Chronic bronchitis is due almost entirely to cigarette smoking. Emphysema is also marked by severe breathlessness and is due to destruction and damage of the air sacs in the lungs. It too is nearly always the result of smoking.

Asthma and pregnancy

Asthma due to allergies often gets better during pregnancy. Other types of asthma are less predictable. They may improve, get worse or stay the same. Look after your asthma carefully during pregnancy, and visit the doctor more frequently. If asthma is going to be a problem during pregnancy, this usually becomes obvious by the fourth month. Each pregnancy tends to follow the pattern of the previous one. Up to a third of women with asthma notice worsening during the week before their periods. The contraceptive pill does not seem to make any difference. This sort of 'premenstrual asthma' often clears up during pregnancy.

Are asthma drugs safe during pregnancy?

Stick rigidly to aerosol treatment if your doctor advises, as these are safe. Steroid tablets are probably harmless, but even so they are best avoided if possible. However, do not stop taking them if your doctor thinks you need them. Remember that severe asthma attacks can be hazardous to your baby.

Allergic broncho-pulmonary aspergillosis

This complicated name is a rare form of asthma due to allergy to a particular sort of fungus called *Aspergillus*. The spores are everywhere in the air we breathe, but fortunately only a few people develop allergy to them. They get asthma but in addition they may have fevers, shadows on their chest X-rays and may cough up thick rubbery lumps of phlegm. The reason for mentioning this condition is that if untreated it can lead to permanent lung damage (more so than severe asthma on its own). Steroid tablets are often needed to clear it up.

Childhood asthma

In the rest of this chapter we will concentrate on children and how asthma affects them. Asthma is the commonest chronic illness in children. About 5–10 per cent of children will have asthma at some stage, but the vast majority have it mildly and are not much troubled by it. Even so, as there are about half a million asthmatic children between five and fourteen years of age in England and Wales, asthma in children accounts for a lot of illness and it is said that 20–30 per cent of time lost at school is due to asthma. Much of this illness may be unnecessary, and is often due to failure to recognize asthma as the cause of the trouble and then failure to treat it properly. It must be stressed that the outlook for children who have asthma is usually very good, and that the aim of treatment is to remove symptoms completely if possible so that the child can enjoy a completely normal life. Only an unlucky few (perhaps 2 per cent of all asthmatic children) with very bad asthma have restriction and disability with everyday activities, and only a tiny number are permanently ill with asthma.

Is childhood asthma due to allergy?

As we mentioned earlier in this chapter, it is not easy to give a clear answer. Certainly allergy plays a more important part in childhood asthma than in adults. Over 90 per cent of asthmatic children have a positive skin test to a common allergen, but this does not mean that 90 per cent of asthma in children is due to allergy. A whole variety of other things can also trigger attacks, just as they can in adults. These are mainly respiratory infections (colds and flu), exercise and sometimes emotional factors. Even if the asthma is mainly allergic, these other things may also trigger attacks at times.

Patterns of asthma in children

Obviously wheeze and breathlessness are the commonest symptoms, and these may be worst at night and disturb sleep. Sometimes coughing at night may be the only symptom and this is where the diagnosis may be missed, as there is little or no wheeze. This type of asthmatic coughing can be very persistent and troublesome, but clears up very well with asthma medicines. On the other hand, not all wheezes are due to asthma. Severe throat infections or the inhalation of a foreign body like a peanut may cause severe wheezing sounds with breathlessness.

Asthma can start at any time in childhood from early infancy to adolescence, but if a child is going to be asthmatic, the first attack is likely in the first few years of life. Twenty-five per cent of asthmatic children start by one year of age, 50 per cent by three years, 80 per cent by five years and only about 5 per cent after eight years. Asthma is twice as common in boys as it is in girls, whereas in adults there is no sex difference.

Children with asthma often have allergic relatives, and many children also have eczema or allergic rhinitis as well. Some have chronic nose or sinus problems. Three-quarters of childhood asthmatics have asthma mildly. This type is easily controlled by bronchodilators.

Wheezy bronchitis or asthma?

There is often confusion about whether a baby or child has asthma or 'wheezy bronchitis'. Often doctors say a child has wheezy bronchitis to avoid using the word 'asthma' because this might upset the parents. This is silly, as the word should now lose its former stigma because of the enormous improvements in treatment.

So are all wheezy babies and children really asthmatics? Probably not. Babies and small children may only get wheezy and breathless with viral infections like colds and flu and may never have another attack. It is thought that this condition, due to germs causing inflammation and narrowing of the baby's already rather small bronchial tubes, is separate from asthma, but as we have said, the two are easily confused. For instance, only 5 per cent of babies under one year old with wheezy bronchitis ever have asthma later on, yet about 40 per cent of 'wheezy bronchitics' over three years of age will turn out to really have asthma. Clearly there is an overlap here, so while you should not immediately assume your baby is asthmatic if wheezing starts during a cold, persistent wheezing attacks may be asthmatic and respond well to treatment.

Treatment

The aims of treatment are the same as for asthma at any age, namely to eliminate breathlessness and wheeze. Remember that a common mistake is a tendency to under-use treatment. The same medicines for adult asthma are generally used. So for mild infrequent attacks, a bronchodilator aerosol like Ventolin is usually enough. For more persistent trouble, sodium cromoglycate is often used next by doctors and is effective in some cases. It only works if taken three to four times daily. Its great advantage is that it has virtually no side effects, although it makes a few children cough. Aminophylline tablets can be used, but are not very popular among doctors in the UK because of troublesome side effects like nausea and vomiting. In the USA they are used a lot. For more severe asthma, steroid aerosols are usually very effective, but only work if taken regularly. Side effects are minimal. Only for very severe chronic asthma or bad attacks are oral steroids needed, and then usually just for short periods.

DESENSITIZATION INJECTIONS

In Chapter 5 we saw that these are probably best reserved for very special cases only. Desensitization to house dust mites or pollen may work in a few cases, but drug treatment is more likely to be effective.

IMMUNIZATIONS AND ALLERGIC CHILDREN

While we are on the subject of injections, which immunizations are safe for allergic children? Some vaccines against virus diseases such as flu, measles and German measles are made in chicken eggs. Although purified, these vaccines may contain minute amounts of egg and may cause reactions in children allergic to egg or feathers. Other vaccines such as tetanus, diphtheria, pertussis (whooping cough), BCG (for TB) and oral polio vaccine are fine for allergic children. Smallpox vaccination used to be avoided in children with eczema, but smallpox has now been eradicated so vaccination is no longer necessary. Flu vaccination is a good idea if there is an epidemic on the way, as a bad attack can affect the lungs and it is worth avoiding the risk if you or your child have asthma. The same applies to whooping cough and measles, which can also affect the lungs, and so vaccination is particularly recommended for asthmatic children. The risks of whooping cough inoculation are now regarded as being far less than the risk of getting the disease itself.

DIETS AND ASTHMA

Complicated exclusion diets make life far too difficult and are usually ignored by children anyway. Whether they are beneficial or not is unproven. If there is an obvious food allergy, for example if severe attacks follow eating eggs, then clearly they should be excluded from the diet. If an exclusion diet is thought to be producing only minor benefit it is often a lot easier to scrap the diet and take a bit more medication.

EXERCISE AND ASTHMA

Up to 90 per cent of children with asthma find that some forms of exercise make the asthma worse. Even laughing can provoke an attack. For some children this is a great problem, as they cannot play sports or even run around the playground. This aspect, often overlooked by parents and teachers, leads to social isolation yet can usually be remedied once identified. Exercise is an important part of any child's physical and social development and so should be encouraged. Firstly, good general control of the asthma should be secured by regular medication. Then, 10–15 minutes before sport or exercise is about to start, an extra dose of sodium cromoglycate or bronchodilator should be inhaled. This will often prevent the attack. Exercise on cold days is particularly likely to provoke attacks. A gentle warm-up period before sports may help. Swimming and gym are less likely to trigger attacks than running. Generally exercise will be beneficial, and not detrimental provided it is not allowed to provoke severe attacks. It allows a child to be normal and boosts self-confidence. Remember that there are several world-class athletes and sportsmen who are asthmatic, who have conquered their asthma so that it does not interfere with their performance.

EMOTION AND STRESS

There is no doubt that emotional upsets can trigger attacks in children with asthma, yet no one believes any longer that psychological factors can actually *cause* the asthma. Some children can become manipulative as a result, and can actually put attacks on at will if they do not get their own way. This can make discipline difficult, make mothers anxious and over-protective, and result in a spoilt child. As far as possible, avoid being blackmailed into granting special favours. Do not let your child use asthma as a weapon. One manoeuvre is to treat the attacks and then discipline your child in the normal way when the attack is controlled.

More deep-seated emotional problems in a child or within the family are more difficult to sort out. These may lead to chronic anxiety in parents and children alike, and can cause problems with children refusing to take medicines regularly. Expert help and advice is often needed. Chronic asthma is an unpleasant disease to have, and taking medicines several times a day is a bore. It is hardly surprising that children often become frustrated, upset and angry. This hostility is often directed at their parents or the doctor, who may seem powerless to help. If asthma cannot be well controlled, the scene is set for behaviour disturbance and other problems. The key usually is to hit the asthma hard with treatment. Very often, if the asthma can be well controlled, the emotional problems will gradually settle. Good control is also important, as time off sick from school means that education suffers.

Before the new effective treatments for asthma were available, bad asthmatics were often sent to special boarding schools where their asthma improved. It was also noticed that being away from home at an ordinary boarding school helped in many cases. Whether those improvements were due to escaping from emotional problems at home or escaping from allergens in the home environment is not clear. On the whole, if your child can attend a normal school, so much the better. The vast majority of asthmatics can. It is very important that the teachers understand about asthma so that your child will take medication regularly. Often teachers are not told that they have an asthmatic child in the class, so make sure that they know. Also, it is probably best if your child takes responsibility for his or her treatment as soon as possible. For a few very severe cases a special school may be the answer, as less schooling will be missed in the long term. Parents often notice an improvement in a child's asthma during holidays taken abroad. Should you consider emigrating? Although there may be an initial improvement in the asthma, it may come back after the move. Asthma is a world-wide disease and crops up in all countries. Finally, remember that improvements in your child's asthma may simply be because he or she has 'grown out' of it.

Do children grow out of asthma?

Several studies have been done to see if asthma improves as children grow up. Many cases of childhood asthma, whether mild or severe, clear up. About half of all cases will be free of asthma altogether by twenty years of age and stay clear, a quarter will clear up but then return later in life, and the rest will carry on having asthma. Some, particularly those still having frequent attacks at fourteen, may get worse as early adult life approaches. Mild asthma is more likely to clear up than severe. Sixty per cent of mild asthmatics will be asthma-free by the age of twenty-one, but only 20 per cent of severe asthmatics will be.

Asthma and your child's career

With luck your child will grow out of asthma and will be able to take on any career. If the asthma lingers, then common sense is needed in choosing a job or career. Environments likely to trigger attacks should be avoided. This may mean that certain occupations are not suitable. For example, if your child is allergic to animals he may have problems being a vet. Other occupations such as working in a bar, in a hairdresser's, in very bad weather, or on a farm may be unsuitable. Deep-sea diving is out for severe asthmatics.

Who should look after your child's asthma?

The best person for this is of course your own family doctor. If your child has severe or complicated asthma, your doctor may refer your child to a childhood asthma clinic if there is one in your area. For severe and sudden attacks either your own doctor will visit or you may go to your local accident and emergency department at the hospital. If you also take your child to the asthma clinic, this may have the advantage that the same team of doctors will treat the acute attacks.

How should your child take the treatment?

Follow your doctor's directions closely. This will ensure best results. Remember that bronchodilator aerosols only last for 3–4 hours, so the dose may need to be repeated. Remember that medicines that prevent attacks, such as sodium cromoglycate and aerosol steroids, are useless unless taken regularly. If your child always gets attacks following colds, then start the treatment at the first sign of an infection. It is easier to nip asthma in the bud. Always have the medication with you. If you go away for the weekend or on holiday, take supplies – do not get caught out in the middle of nowhere on a Sunday night. Most children are not hypersensitive to aspirin but it is best avoided even so, particularly as it may be associated with the rare but serious condition Reye's syndrome. Use paracetamol syrup (e.g. Calpol) instead. Give medication regularly, though it is unnecessary to wake a peacefully sleeping, comfortably breathing child in the middle of the night. If your child is on a lot of medication, do not stop suddenly simply because the asthma has improved. There may be a rebound effect with worsening asthma. Discuss it with your doctor. Generally, treatment should be reduced gradually.

Problems giving medicine to children

Children generally hate having things squirted up their noses or down their throats. A lot of persuasion, coaxing and even bribery may be needed until a child has got used to taking a spray or aerosol and realizes the benefit. Pills and tablets can be difficult too, but pills are easier to swallow when lying down than when sitting up. Try giving your child the pill followed by a mouthful of water, then get him or her to lie down. This should do the trick. Grinding pills up and concealing them in food often fails if the bitter taste comes through. Most medicines that have to be taken by mouth are also available as syrups and elixirs, which are much easier for children to take.

Are breathing exercises helpful?

Some children may be helped by being taught how to breathe in a relaxed way, using the lower ribs and focusing more on breathing out than breathing in.

How do I know if my child is having a severe attack?

A distressed, irritable, anxious child who cannot complete a sentence because of rapid difficult breathing and is obviously fighting for breath or who looks blue should be taken immediately to the nearest hospital. Call an ambulance.

Apart from hopefully very rare major attacks like this (the risk of which will be much less if you ensure that your child takes regular treatment as directed by your doctor), you may find that it is useful to have your own peak flow meter so that you can measure your child's peak flows at home and so get an early warning if things are going wrong.

If your child has an attack, give an extra dose of the bronchodilator aerosol first. Do *not* give sedatives. Keep calm and maintain a confident exterior. Panic, fear and anxiety are easily transmitted to children.

Above all, if you are unhappy about the way things are going or do not think that things are under control, then call the doctor or go to the hospital. It is far better to err on the side of caution. After all, why should you and your child have sleepless and anxious nights when things could probably be sorted out quite quickly by your doctor or nearest accident department?

Chapter Seven

The Skin

Eczema – what is it?

Eczema, or dermatitis as it is sometimes called, is a skin disease and is probably the result of many different factors. (Actually the term dermatitis is often used rather loosely but strictly just means inflamed skin.) The rash generally looks the same despite the cause, and is the skin's response to a variety of different sorts of insult, just as asthma is the response made by the lung to a whole range of different things.

Eczema is common and it is not infectious. The skin affected is red and inflamed, usually dry and flaky, so that it peels or scales. It is usually very itchy and this encourages scratching. The rash may become thickened and dry and then chap leaving painful cracks, or it may be wet and weepy. It can get infected by germs, particularly if it is scratched a lot. Eczema can affect the skin anywhere on the body, but most commonly it goes for the face, scalp, neck, the creases of the elbows and knees, and around the wrists and ankles. It can be confused with several other skin diseases, for example fungal infections.

The whole subject of eczema is complicated and confusing and is not yet fully worked out. If you are a bit muddled after reading the following section, don't worry, everybody is!

Is eczema due to allergies?

Some kinds of eczema are, some kinds are not, some kinds may be.

What kinds of eczema are there?

We will deal only with the main ones here. Sometimes there is a good deal of overlap between the different kinds, so that someone may seem to have an eczema that has features of several different kinds. The difficulty is often to decide what type it is just on its appearance, when the cause is not apparent.

IRRITANT ECZEMA

Anyone whose skin is damaged by a large exposure to an irritant substance will get an irritant eczema. This is not an allergy. Irritant eczema can be caused by exposing the skin to strong acids, detergents and other cleaning agents and various oils. People prone to getting this type are people who do domestic work, chemical workers, hairdressers and so on. People's skin sensitivity varies, so that some are more likely to get this type of eczema than others.

CONTACT ECZEMA

This kind of eczema is due to an allergic reaction to things that contact the skin.

ATOPIC ECZEMA

This condition may be related to allergy but it is not clear exactly how. People with this type often have hayfever and asthma as well.

SEBORRHOEIC ECZEMA

This kind is not due to allergy. Examples are nappy rash and cradle-cap in babies. Adults can get it too, usually in the scalp, on the face and on the trunk.

PHOTO-ALLERGIC ECZEMA

This kind may be due to an allergy. What happens is that a person becomes 'sensitized' by something. This can be a particular food (for example parsnips, figs or celery) or a drug (for example certain antibiotics), or a cream put on the skin, or a perfume or aftershave. When that person is exposed to the ultraviolet rays in sunshine, eczema develops on the areas of skin exposed.

OTHER SORTS OF ECZEMA

There are other sorts, none being due to allergy. Now for details of the two common sorts of eczema.

Contact eczema

This is a skin rash which results directly from contact with often small amounts of a particular substance to which an allergy has developed. Not everyone who is exposed gets it. The allergy is not due to IgE antibody like most other allergies. It is due to T lymphocytes (see Chapters 2 and 3).

WHAT CAUSES CONTACT ECZEMA?

Many substances can sensitize the skin and lead to contact eczema. Some are commoner than others. First, metals can do it. Women are most affected by contact eczema due to nickel, which is used in costume jewellery. It crops up with nickel-containing earrings, necklaces and rings where they contact the skin. Bra-clips, metal buttons or rivets in jeans and coinage can do it too. Chromate is present in cement and can cause problems for construction workers. Many chemicals can cause contact eczema and so cause problems in the home and in industry. Examples are; agents (dichromates) used to tan leather, which may lead to eczema on the feet from shoes, rubber (rubber gloves and wellington boots), various plastics, oils in paints and polishes and, finally, epoxy and acrylic glues. Cosmetics are the next trouble zone. Perfumes, ointments, creams, suntan lotion, hair sprays, dyes and bleaches and scented soaps can all be responsible. Other causes are various antibiotics in ointments, lanolin, and some plants, in particular primula, chrysanthemum and, in the USA, poison ivy.

HOW IS IT DIAGNOSED?

This can be easy and obvious, particularly if the rash is on the body just where your shoe, watchstrap, earring or necklace has been. But it can be very difficult if the rash affects the hands, because our hands are in contact with such a vast array of different things all the time. This is why contact eczema can be such a pest to people who do housework or work in factories with chemicals. There are lots of hazards in the home, garage and garden as well as in factories, with soaps, detergents, cleaning agents, polishes, rubber, plants, cosmetics and so on. Added to which, washing the hands with soap or washing up with detergent constantly de-greases the skin, making it drier and more susceptible.

PATCH TESTS

We have already talked about these. To be useful they should be done by a dermatologist. The aim is to identify the allergen causing the trouble so that it can then be avoided. Small amounts of the suspect substances are put on to the skin under airtight dressings and are examined 2–4 days later. Often a battery of twenty or so common culprits are put on at one sitting. The substance causing the contact eczema will have produced a patch of eczema when the dressings are removed.

HOW IS CONTACT ECZEMA TREATED?

The first rule is to avoid any further contact with the allergen causing the eczema if this can be identified. This may be easier said than done. It is quite easy to stop wearing nickel-containing jewellery, but other substances are very widespread and are difficult to avoid. More than one may be responsible, and not all may have been identified either by obvious reactions on contact or by patch-testing.

General measures that may help will be to avoid excessive wetting of the hands or other affected skin and to avoid exposure to any of the irritants we have already mentioned which are likely to stir things up. This may mean wearing protective clothes or rubber gloves (provided you are not allergic to rubber!). Lined plastic gloves are available. Also, protect the skin and minimize cuts and grazes, as trauma to the skin will tend to stir the eczema up. Emollient creams and ointments moisten the skin and prevent chapping. Steroid creams and ointments may be needed, particularly if the hands or feet are badly affected.

WHAT IS THE LONG-TERM OUTLOOK?

Generally unpredictable. Once contact eczema to a substance has developed, the sensitivity to it can last a lifetime. Certainly contact eczema can be very persistent and a real nuisance particularly if it affects the hands. In cases where the allergen can be identified and meticulously avoided, the skin can return to normal. Sometimes it is not possible to avoid the allergen even when it has been identified – if it is an essential part of a job that cannot be given up, for example.

Atopic eczema

WHAT IS IT?

This type of eczema is commoner in young children. Up to 3 per cent get it. It usually starts during the first six months of life, although it can develop at any age. It is called 'atopic' eczema because it is commoner in children who have various allergies anyway, in particular, allergic rhinitis or asthma. (Atopic means roughly the same thing as allergic; see Chapter 3.) It also tends to develop in the children of allergic parents more than in those of non-allergic parents. About 50 per cent of children with atopic eczema have asthma or allergic rhinitis as well, whereas 60 per cent of children with troublesome asthma also have eczema. Children with both asthma and eczema tend to swap one for the other; when the asthma is bad the eczema clears up, and when the asthma is good, the eczema flares up again.

IS ATOPIC ECZEMA DUE TO ALLERGY?

The cause of atopic eczema is unknown. Generally, it occurs in allergic people and accompanies allergic asthma or rhinitis, but whether the rash itself is due to allergy is uncertain. The connection between the two is confusing and controversial, and not nearly as clear as the connection between allergy and rhinitis for example. To start with, the antibody IgE is very often present in large amounts in the blood, and the skin tests are often positive in atopic eczema. But there is little or no connection between these and the severity of the eczema. It has been suggested that allergy to house dust mites may be important, but this is controversial. Although IgE is increased in amounts, it seems to play no part in the inflammation that leads to the skin rash. Also, in people who have atopic eczema but do not have asthma or rhinitis, the skin tests may all be negative. Finally, there is no clear-cut connection between being exposed to an allergen – say pollen – and coming out in an eczema rash.

SO WHAT CAUSES IT?

No one knows – yet. But some cases are definitely made worse by various things such as stress, emotional upset, teething in infants, excessive heat, sweating a lot, excessive dryness of the skin and scratching. General irritants like detergents and scented soaps may stir it up. Some find wool or nylon against the skin is bad. Skin infections or coughs and colds may provoke attacks, particularly in children. Undoubtedly some children's eczema is much worse when pets are around. It is worth being on the lookout for things that contact your skin which seem to make the eczema worse, and avoiding them if you can.

DIET AND ATOPIC ECZEMA

Whether diet is important in atopic eczema remains a subject of hot dispute among experts. Some say yes, some say no. In some cases intolerance of or allergy to a substance in the diet may be involved, but this is probably important only in a small number of people with atopic dermatitis.

Some babies and infants are allergic or intolerant to hen's eggs and cow's milk. Allergy to eggs and to cow's milk is frequently connected to atopic eczema in infants. It is often noticed that eczema develops when breast-feeding is stopped and the baby starts on other foods. Milk and egg allergy seem to be the most common, but allergies to cereals, nuts and fish may also be important.

Some studies have shown that if eggs and cow's milk are totally excluded from the diet, atopic eczema in very young children will improve in the majority of cases, but other studies show little or no improvement. Certainly a minority of people find that dietary components make their eczema or their child's eczema worse, but most find that diet makes no difference. In addition to eggs and milk, nuts, fish and cereals, the sort of things that make some people's eczema worse are spicy food like curries, alcoholic drinks, and certain dyes, such as tartrazine, used to colour food and drinks. To sum up, diet probably makes no difference to the vast majority of people with atopic eczema, except to some small children with cow's milk or egg sensitivity.

HOW DOES ATOPIC ECZEMA USUALLY BEHAVE?

As we have said, it usually starts between the age of three and six months, but can start at any time. It often starts on the cheeks, then spreads to the rest of the face, the eyebrows and the forehead. The scalp and nappy area may also be affected. Later on it can spread to the creases at the elbows and knees, around the wrists, ankles, ears and eyes. The trunk can be involved too. Where the rash affects creases or points of friction, the skin can get thickened and form painful cracks. If the rash is scratched a lot it can get infected.

The rash usually comes and goes of its own accord in an unpredictable manner. Most infants grow out of it. It is usually clearing by the second or third birthday, and is gone in most children by the age of seven years. If it is still present at puberty it may still clear up then, but in some cases it can get worse. But the earlier atopic eczema starts and the more severe it is, the more likely it is to carry on. About a quarter of kids with severe atopic eczema will still have it as adults. Mild cases do much better.

WHAT CAN YOU DO TO MINIMIZE ATOPIC ECZEMA?

Breast-feeding is probably a good idea, and some experts say it should be continued for as long as possible particularly if the parents have allergies. But even this is controversial. Others say that breast-feeding merely delays the onset of eczema in those who are destined to get it anyway, and that all babies have to start on solids some time.

What about excluding eggs and cow's milk from the diet? As we have said, this may improve a few cases. But egg is difficult to exclude because it is used so much in cooking, and cow's milk substitutes like goat's milk or soya bean milk can cause allergies too.

General measures that may help are to avoid undue stress or emotional upsets, to avoid wool or nylon clothes next to the skin if they make the rash worse, and to avoid strong detergents and bleaches to wash clothes, as this may stir things up. Many people find that cotton clothing is most comfortable. Be careful what you get on your skin. Detergents, scented soap, paints, oils, cosmetics may all irritate and make the rash dry and sore. Excessive bathing of children with lots of soap may also lead to a dry irritable skin. Finally – don't scratch! Cut your child's fingernails short. Mittens at night may work. It may be pretty well impossible to stop children scratching altogether without it becoming a major focus for confrontation, so try and reduce the damage at least.

WHAT TESTS ARE HELPFUL?

Skin tests may be positive (often to pollen and house dust mite), especially in cases who also have asthma or rhinitis. They are not helpful in diagnosis or treatment.

In some cases, if the dermatologist suspects that you or your child has contact eczema rather than, or as well as, atopic eczema, he may arrange patch-testing for you.

WHAT THEN IS THE TREATMENT OF ATOPIC ECZEMA?

Avoiding allergens including dietary components does not usually improve this type of eczema, except in some babies with egg or milk intolerance. This is not a great surprise, as the relation between this type of eczema and allergy is very vague. For the same reason, most agree that desensitization injections are useless.

Avoiding skin irritants, on the other hand, will help. Use simple soap to wash. Avoid scented soap, detergents and chemicals.

Taking regular baths is probably helpful in most cases. Avoid lengthy baths as these tend to aggravate skin dryness. Use plain soap sparingly. Dry yourself adequately. Oilatum emollient is an emollient oil which can be added to the bathwater. This will keep the skin moist, soothed and flexible. Do not use bubble bath or similar solutions which are too strong, and do not use very hot water.

Emulsifying ointment and aqueous cream are bland agents to put on the skin to moisten, soothe and reduce itching and cracking of the skin. They should be applied at least twice a day. The trouble is they are a bit messy.

Itching leads to scratching and scratching damages the skin, which may then get infected. Itching can be reduced by mild sedative antihistamine drugs. These may be particularly useful if taken at bed-time to ensure a good night's sleep.

Steroid ointments and creams have revolutionized the treatment of eczema, very much as steroid aerosols have revolutionized asthma. Hydrocortisone ointment or cream is available in various strengths. Stronger steroids like betnovate or dermovate are also used. Which one you use and for how long will be determined by your doctor. Follow his or her instructions carefully for best results. Steroids do not cure eczema, they just damp it down, but as eczema is inclined to come and go of its own accord you may not need to use steroids all the time. If the eczema is very severe, your doctor may recommend a spell in hospital for intensive treatment to get things under control. It is important to find out from the doctor just how creams and ointments should be applied and if they should be covered by dressings or not. Generally, steroid ointments are better than creams, as they moisturize the skin more, but they are a bit more messy. But if the rash is very inflamed or is weeping and infected, creams are more soothing. If the rash does get infected your doctor may prescribe a steroid cream containing an antiseptic, or you may need a course of antibiotic tablets.

Urticaria

WHAT IS IT?

Urticaria is the medical word for the itchy skin swellings of nettle rash or hives. The skin becomes itchy and a white raised area appears, surrounded by reddening of the skin. Urticaria may occur in crops over any part of the body, and attacks may last from a few hours to several days. The lumps are often circular in shape and resemble insect bites or nettle stings, but they can affect much larger areas of skin as well. Urticaria also looks a bit like the positive skin tests we talked about earlier, in fact an injection of histamine into the skin will result in an itchy lump identical to urticaria. Urticaria can come on suddenly, following an exposure to something that triggers it off, or crops of urticaria can keep recurring in attacks over months or even years without any apparent cause. Urticaria is quite common, and about one person in ten will have it at some time.

IS URTICARIA DUE TO ALLERGIES?

There are many causes of urticaria. Allergies to various things definitely account for some cases, but by no means all. Urticaria can be triggered off by a wide range of other things besides allergies. The skin tests are often all negative in urticaria. Even so, urticaria is probably more common in people with allergies. For example, about 20 per cent of hayfever sufferers have urticaria as well at some stage. Urticaria is also quite common in people with atopic eczema.

HOW DOES AN ATTACK OF URTICARIA HAPPEN?

Whatever triggers it off, the blood vessel capillaries in the affected skin become leaky so that there is an outpouring of fluid into the tissue just below the skin's surface. This makes it swell up. The blood supply to the affected area is increased, so the skin gets red and inflamed. These changes are due to release of the mediators of inflammation (like histamine) from mast cells in the skin, which also gives rise to intense itching. As we have already seen, mast cells can be triggered by allergens if they are coated in IgE antibody. This accounts for the allergic type of urticaria. But mast cells can also be triggered in other ways without involving IgE antibody at all. This may account for the cases of urticaria that do not seem to be allergic.

ALLERGIC URTICARIA

First of all let us deal with urticaria that is definitely due to allergies. This type usually happens in sharp short bursts following exposure to allergens. The commonest allergens to cause urticaria are pollen and various animals, particularly cats, and various foods. The victims are usually young children, often with other allergies as well. Of foods, eggs and milk are the commonest causes, and children generally grow out of this type of urticaria. Some of these children may have atopic eczema too. Sometimes a food allergic child will develop swelling of the lips and tongue on eating the food, causing the allergy local urticaria. Vomiting may then follow. As the allergen is absorbed into the blood stream, generalized urticaria may develop all over the body. Skin tests to food allergens may be positive in this type. Other foods that cause this type of urticaria are fish, nuts, shellfish, some fruits and some vegetables. Allergic urticaria can start later in life as well. It may appear for the first time during pregnancy or following a viral infection. Finally, there are two very important causes of allergic urticaria: allergy to various drugs like penicillin and other antibiotics and bee and wasp stings. We will deal with these later.

CONTACT URTICARIA

This is urticaria resulting from direct contact of the skin with various things. The sort of things that can cause this type of urticaria are various foods, plants, pets (cats in particular), chemicals and textiles like wool.

PHYSICAL URTICARIA

All sorts of physical events can trigger urticaria in susceptible individuals. These are scratching, direct pressure on the skin, heat, hot baths, cold, exercise, exposure to sunshine or emotional stress. Obviously allergy is not involved here.

ANGIO OEDEMA

This is a rare disorder that affects deep tissues. The same process that causes urticaria is involved. It is generally more severe than urticaria, and attacks consist of widespread swelling of the face, mouth, lips and throat. If the throat is affected it may make breathing difficult, and some cases also get stomach pains due to swellings in the digestive system. Some cases respond to antihistamine drugs, but adrenalin is needed for very severe attacks. A rare form of this disorder is hereditary, that is, it is a lifelong condition; attacks come and go and may be brought on by stress or trauma to tissues. It is not due to an allergy but due to a deficiency of a special substance in the blood.

OTHER CAUSES OF URTICARIA

First, components of the diet may aggravate urticaria and make attacks more frequent. Examples are fish, cheese, yeast, beer and other alcoholic drinks, citrus fruit, chocolate, tomatoes and strawberries. Some drugs, such as aspirin, barbiturate and other pain-killers like morphine and codeine, may trigger attacks.

Some types of chronic urticaria may also be due to preservatives and colouring agents in food. Examples are the azo-dyes such as tartrazine which are used to colour food and drink, and benzoate preservatives used in canned food.

There are two final causes of urticaria. First, it can be caused by infection by parasites and intestinal worms – with the increasing amount of foreign travel and migration, these infestations are being seen more frequently in the UK. Second, very very rarely, urticaria is associated with various internal diseases.

URTICARIA OF UNKNOWN CAUSE

After this long list it will come as a disappointment to hear that in most cases of urticaria no cause is ever found. A cause is more likely to be found in acute urticaria than in the chronic type where attacks go on and on. A cause is finally pinned down (often after careful inquiries) in only about a quarter of cases, and in the majority of cases the cause remains a complete mystery.

HOW CAN THE CAUSE BE FOUND?

First, think carefully to see if any of the things we have mentioned seem to set attacks off, or make them worse. Skin tests are on the whole unhelpful, except for the occasional case due to a food allergy. For severe cases of chronic urticaria some allergists might recommend provocation tests, in which small doses of tartrazine, benzoates, aspirin or yeast are given in turn to see if attacks are provoked. Another and more complicated approach is to take a 'fresh food' only diet, which will be free of colouring and preserving agents, to see if any improvement occurs. Finally, elimination diets consisting of foods least likely to provoke urticaria (for example, lamb, carrots and rice) can be used, and then different foods are introduced one by one to try and identify the cause. All these tests are complicated and troublesome to do, and many feel they are just not worth the effort.

TREATMENT OF URTICARIA

As the cause is often never found, treatment is aimed at suppressing the attacks. This usually means taking antihistamine tablets, which are very effective in most cases. It is obviously important to avoid things which you find trigger attacks off or make them worse. Desensitization injections are unlikely to help, unless the cause of the urticaria is allergy to bee or wasp stings.

WHAT IS THE OUTLOOK?

Good. Half are free of urticaria attacks by one year, most have cleared up by two, but about one in five will still have the odd attack up to ten years later. Urticaria is a nuisance to have and can be unsightly to look at, but it is not actually hazardous to health. Most people with urticaria are completely healthy otherwise.

Chapter Eight

The Digestive System.
Food Intolerance and Food Allergy

The whole business of food intolerance and allergy is fraught with difficulty, and there is endless confusion and argument. We will try and highlight the problem spots. As yet there are no easy solutions to the food allergy problem. The medical profession generally remains sceptical about food allergy, largely because of the absence of firm evidence from clinical studies. This view may well change as research proceeds. At the moment it is often difficult to make a firm diagnosis of food intolerance or allergy, either because the relation between symptoms and eating is vague or because there are not really any accurate tests. Some doctors say food allergy does not exist at all, other practitioners claim that it is the cause of many symptoms and diseases. Research, which may require painstaking trials of dietary exclusion followed by challenge tests, may one day show that food intolerance is responsible for a wider range of problems than we believe now, but certainly at the moment food allergy is blamed far too frequently to explain away various vague symptoms.

Does food allergy really exist?

That food intolerance and allergy really do exist is beyond doubt. The difficulty is how common and how important the problem is. Also, can food intolerance develop to any food or only to some? It is not very surprising that allergy to various foods can develop, in view of the complex job the digestive system has to do in absorbing nutrients yet fending off germs and harmful substances that may also be present in the diet. Even so, most experts think that true food allergy and intolerance is generally rare, and much less common than other types of allergy. When food allergy does crop up, it is commoner in children than in adults and is very often accompanied by other allergies as well.

Before going further we must be clear about exactly what food allergy and intolerance are, and first of all we must deal with food aversion.

Food aversion

This is purely a psychological disgust with a particular food. It may be muddled with food allergy or food intolerance. Just the thought of tripe and onions makes me want to vomit, but if I was fooled into eating tripe disguised as something else, I might even like it. This would not be so if I had food intolerance to tripe – I would be sick just the same. Food aversion is just an intense dislike of a particular food, and if it is forced, vomiting may occur. It is most common in children.

Food allergy

Symptoms follow eating particular foods because of an allergic reaction, usually of the hypersensitivity type involving IgE antibody and mast cells, just like the other allergies we have been discussing. Symptoms usually develop shortly after eating the food, there may be several foods to which allergy develops, and very often food allergy victims have other allergies as well, for example to pollen, dust mites or cats.

Food intolerance

Food intolerance is much more common than true food allergy. Again, particular foods may be involved and provoke symptoms but *not* by a reaction involving IgE antibody as far as we can tell. The particular food producing the intolerance has a direct irritant effect of some sort in susceptible individuals every time it is eaten.

Food intolerance versus food allergy

Obviously these two are closely linked in some ways, as rather similar symptoms are produced after eating certain foods. Generally, in food intolerance, symptoms occur only in the digestive system, but in food allergy, symptoms involving the nose, lungs and skin often develop as well. With food allergy, there is nothing wrong with the food, it is the allergic response to it that causes the trouble. With food intolerance, it is substances in the food that cause harm, usually in someone who has an abnormal sensitivity to those substances (for reasons we do not really understand). A further link between food intolerance and food allergy is that when you look at the lists of foods that cause the reactions, the same food can cause both types of reaction – allergy or intolerance. In many other cases no one has shown whether a particular food or additive produces its undesirable effects by intolerance or by allergy.

What are the symptoms of food allergy and intolerance?

As there is so much overlap in symptoms caused by allergy and those caused by intolerance, we will consider them together. First, symptoms can come on almost immediately after eating often only tiny amounts of the offending item, and this can make the diagnosis obvious. The cause is often a food allergy, and the skin tests or RAST test may be positive. Treatment is easy. Just avoid that particular food. On the other hand, symptoms can be delayed up to twelve or even thirty-six hours after eating the food. Symptoms are often vague, and the food causing it is frequently eaten and often in large amounts. The diagnosis may not be at all obvious and is often made only with certainty by dietary exclusion. Skin tests are usually negative.

Digestive system symptoms

These are most commonly nausea, vomiting and diarrhoea. Abdominal pain, bloating of the abdomen and wind may also occur. Constipation is more unusual. In very severe cases, fainting and collapse may occur. When the food is taken into the mouth, swelling of the lips and throat may occur, with tingling and discomfort. All these may come on very suddenly after eating the food.

More persistent symptoms, when the food is taken every day (for example cow's milk intolerance in infants), include chronic vomiting and diarrhoea, and failure to put on weight.

Other symptoms

True food allergy very often gives symptoms outside the digestive system as well. In one study, about 60 per cent of cases also had eczema or asthma and a further 30 per cent also had urticaria or rhinitis, so that only 10 per cent had symptoms in the digestive system alone. Food intolerance, on the other hand, is inclined to give symptoms only in the digestive system. Purely 'subjective' symptoms without any digestive symptoms, such as fatigue, feeling generally off colour, restlessness, and depression, are thought to be very rare in food allergy and intolerance and are much more likely to be due to neurosis or other psychological disturbance.

Many other vague symptoms have been attributed to food allergy and intolerance, but it is hard to prove one way or the other. These include behaviour and mood disturbance in infants with cow's milk intolerance, hyperactivity in children, headaches, mouth ulcers, generalized aches and pains and arthritis. We will talk about these later on.

To sum up, symptoms either come on quickly and suggest the cause (vomiting, diarrhoea, pain, asthma, urticaria, rhinitis, eczema), or they are more persistent due to eating the food all the time (chronic diarrhoea, and weight loss, for example).

Causes of food intolerance and allergy

As there is so much overlap between food allergy and intolerance as far as the effects they produce are concerned, we will lump all the causes together (see Table 2 on page 140).

Table 2   Causes of Food Intolerance and Allergy

COMMON CAUSES

Milk and milk products (e.g. cheeses)
Egg
Nuts (peanuts particularly)
Fish (e.g. tuna, mackerel)
Shellfish (shrimps, crab, lobster)

LESS COMMON

Wheat/flour/cereals/yeast/yeast extract/baked products
Seafood – squid, clam, oysters, mussels, and other seafood
Vegetables – celery, artichoke, peas, beans, soya, tomato, peppers, avocado
Alcoholic drinks – beer, red wine
Fruit – citrus fruit, berry fruit, apple, banana, pineapple
Meat – pork, bacon, chicken, tenderized meat
Chocolate, coffee, tea
Additives – see table 3 on page 144
Spices and herbs – see below

FOODS LEAST LIKELY TO CAUSE ALLERGY OR INTOLERANCE

Rice	Carrots
Barley	Lamb
Lettuce	Potato
Grapes	

HERBS AND SPICES THAT MAY CAUSE INTOLERANCE REACTIONS

Cinnamon	Fennel
Cloves	Garlic
Horseradish	Bay
Mustard	Thyme
Sesame	Sage
Caraway	Nutmeg

First of all, food may contain various poisons or germs that produce upset. Food that is 'off' may contain germs that lead to violent vomiting and diarrhoea and abdominal pain (gastro-enteritis), for example. Mouldy peanuts and some types of beans if undercooked contain poisons which cause trouble. Some foods contain chemicals that are not poisonous but will produce symptoms in sensitive people. Tea and coffee contain caffeine. Some people find that too much tea or coffee makes them feel anxious or stops them sleeping. Others notice racing and thumping of the heart, shaking, nausea and even vomiting. Some foods contain substances called amines, which have various adverse effects in sensitive people. Examples are tyramine which is plentiful in some cheeses, some red wine and chocolate, and histamine which can be present in high amounts in fish, canned foods and cheese. Other foods like egg white, shellfish and strawberries do not contain much histamine themselves but in some people actually trigger histamine release from the digestive system lining and so produce symptoms. Examples of other amine-containing foods are beef and yeast extracts, broad beans, pineapple, tomato, banana and avocado. Big doses of these amines lead to throbbing headaches, or even migraine, flushing, sweating, palpitation and general discomfort. The flavour enhancer monosodium glutamate, which is used extensively in Chinese cooking, can give alarming symptoms if taken in large quantities. Headaches, pains in the chest, a racing thumping heart-beat, marked weakness and difficulty in breathing can be severe enough to be confused with a heart attack after large Chinese meals. Sometimes there is intolerance or allergy to several foods, and these may be related, that is, a person may be allergic to peas and beans. Other people may be allergic to something when it is raw but not when it is cooked. People can be intolerant to fatty foods and always feel sick and bloated after a fried meal of meat, whereas others are ill after spicy foods or curries. Spices and curries are irritating to the lining of the digestive system, and sensitive people cannot take them.

On rare occasions the digestive system lacks an enzyme that is important in breaking down a particular food in preparation for its absorption. The commonest of these rare defects is where the enzyme necessary to break down the sugar in milk is missing. This means that the milk-sugar is not broken down, which in turn leads to diarrhoea. This happens mainly in infants. Either they are just born with the defect, or they develop it temporarily after a bad attack of gastro-enteritis, which damages the digestive system lining so that it loses this important enzyme. Either way, this lack of enzyme is one of the causes of intolerance to cow's milk in infants. The other cause is true allergy to cow's milk, where IgE antibodies develop.

Apart from milk, severe allergies can develop to eggs, nuts, fish and shellfish and more rarely to yeast, cereals, fruits and vegetables. Alcoholic drinks can cause problems in several ways. First, as we have said, some (particularly red wine) contain the amine tyramine. All alcoholic drinks are fermented with yeast, so that yeast-allergic people may be unable to take them. Fizzy alcoholic drinks such as beer, cider, champagne and sparkling wine contain more yeast than spirits such as vodka and gin, which can be tolerated by some yeast-allergic people who cannot take beer. Other people are allergic to additional components in alcoholic drinks, such as colouring and preserving agents.

Causes in children

As we have said, food allergy or intolerance is commonest in children under three years. It usually passes off as the child gets older, and by far the commonest causes are allergy or intolerance to cow's milk and eggs. There is much disagreement as to exactly how common this condition is, and it may be as many as one child in twenty who is affected. Following a meal of milk or eggs, vomiting and diarrhoea may be accompanied by urticaria, rhinitis and asthma. Children under three years may also be intolerant to nuts (especially peanuts) and soya. Children over three years can have troubles with milk, eggs, nuts and soya as well, but this is less common. Intolerance and allergy to milk nearly always clears up, but allergy to nuts may go on into adult life.

Food additives, allergy and intolerance

The final group of substances that may cause food intolerance or allergy are the food additives. Again, there is much argument as to how important they really are as a cause of intolerance. Some say that intolerance rarely if ever occurs, others say that additives in food are an important cause of much ill health. As usual, evidence one way or the other is hard to come by. Certainly, on what evidence is available, intolerance to these substances seems to be very rare. Food intolerance itself is rare, and intolerance to additives is even more rare. A recent survey suggested that between one in 1,000 and one in 10,000 children had intolerance to a food additive. Nevertheless there is enormous interest and concern about additives at the moment, so we will go into some detail.

Food additives and E numbers (see Table 3 on page 144)

Since time immemorial man has added substances to food to preserve or flavour it. Meat was preserved by salting it, its flavour improved by spices, and fruit was preserved by the addition of syrup. Nowadays, much of our food is processed and contains various additives. For example, some cheeses contain up to ten additives including preservatives, emulsifiers and stabilizers and colouring agents. The shelf-life of many foods and drinks is greatly increased by the addition of preservatives and antioxidants. These are agents which deter the growth of germs and so stop food going bad. The commonly used preservatives are nitrites and nitrates, benzoates, sulphur dioxide and sulphites, acetic and lactic acid. The antioxidants, for example vitamin E and butylated hydroxyanisole, prevent fats from becoming rancid and are used in many foods such as ice cream, crisps, drinks and cereals. Emulsifiers, stabilizers and thickeners such as pectins, alginates and gums are added to improve the consistency and texture of food. A wide range of colouring agents make food and drink look more attractive, and various artificial agents are added to improve and enhance flavour. Tenderizing, curing and spicing agents are used particularly in processed meat and fish. Finally, poultry, milk, meat and fish may be affected by what the animal was fed on. Animal feeds may contain steroids or antibiotics if these were used to improve growth. Recent concern about additives is connected with the possibility, not only that these additives may cause allergies and intolerance, but also that they may cause a wide range of other

Table 3   Examples of Food Additives

COLOURING AGENTS

Tartrazine	E102
Quinoline yellow	E104
Yellow 2G	E107
Sunset Yellow	E110
Azorubine	E122
Amaranth	E123
Ponceau 4R	E124
Erythrocine BS	E127
Red 2G	E128
Brilliant blue FCF	E133
Green S	E142

PRESERVATIVES

Sorbates	E200–203
Benzoates	E210–219
Sulphur dioxide & Sulphites	E220–227
Nitrites & Nitrates	E249–252

ANTIOXIDANTS

Ascorbic acid and derivatives (vitamin C)	E300–304
Vitamin E & derivatives	E306–309
Butylated hydroxyanisole	E320
Butylated hydroxytoluene	E321

SWEETENERS AND FLAVOURINGS

Sorbitol	E420
Glutamic acid	E620
Monosodium glutamate	E621
Quinine	
Vanilla	

OTHERS

Emulsifiers and stabilizers – Lecithins	E322
Enzyme meat tenderizers – Papain	

EXAMPLES OF HARMLESS NATURALLY OCCURRING ADDITIVES

Riboflavin	E101	Vitamin C	E300
Caramel	E150	Vitamin E	E306
Calcium carbonate	E170	Citric acid	E330
Acetic acid	E260	Nicotinic acid	E375
Lactic acid	E270	Beeswax	E901
Carbon dioxide	E290		

diseases as well and that some may even cause cancer. The trend, as a result of much publicized research over the last twenty years (as we mentioned earlier), has been towards a major change in our diets. A major swing towards high fibre, low animal fat diets is under way throughout much of the Western world, as people become increasingly aware that low fibre, high animal fat and high carbohydrate diets are being incriminated as increasing the risk of getting a whole host of diseases, including heart attacks, varicose veins, bowel cancer, haemorrhoids and diabetes. Many people are now looking for a healthier, more natural diet with less processed food in it. 'Junk' food, which is high in additives, fats, salt and carbohydrates, is getting an increasingly bad press and is blamed for all manner of ills, including obesity, heart disease, depression and personality disturbances. Food additives in particular have been blamed for allergies, chronic ill health and hyperactivity in children. One study in particular showed that some hyperactive children improved when they took an additive-free diet. Tartrazine in particular has been singled out as a cause of allergic reactions, including asthma, and of hyperactivity in children. The evidence suggests that about one child in 1,000 is sensitive to tartrazine, and that asthmatic attacks can be provoked by taking it. Whether it really causes hyperactivity is controversial. Tartrazine is an orange dye frequently used to colour fizzy drinks, sweets, cheese, smoked fish, sauces, salad cream, tinned fruit and vegetables. Benzoates, used in preserving food, can produce allergies and intolerant reactions including urticaria and asthma, but they are probably very rare. Nitrite preservatives may produce flushing and faintness. Some of these colouring and flavouring agents are also used in tablets and medicines.

To sum up, on what we know at the moment, most food additives probably only very rarely cause allergic or other untoward reactions. It is highly unlikely that they cause depression, cancer, general ill health, or indigestion. For the vast majority of people they are harmless. In fact some additives are naturally occurring components of food anyway (see Table 3, page 144). Food manufacturers are now required by law to state what additions have been made to their products. Only EEC approved additives are permitted. To avoid long-winded chemical names, these substances are coded and all have an 'E' number (standing for E E C approved) so that you can check exactly what a particular product contains.

Many people are increasingly disturbed by the notion that their food is adulterated with unnecessary additives, and for this reason many food manufacturers are now marketing alternative products that do not contain artificial colouring and flavourings.

But let us remember that preservatives, antioxidants, flavourings, etc. have brought many advantages to our lives, by greatly increasing the range, variety and quality of foods available. Additive-free food would be bland and much of it could not be stored. For example, without preservatives, fish, meat, baked products, beer, soft drinks and sauces would not keep. Without antioxidants, oil-containing foods would go rancid and dried foods like cereals, crisps, and dried milk could not be stored. Without colouring, much food would look greyish and unappealing.

Diagnosis of food allergy and intolerance

The most important factor in diagnosis of food allergy or intolerance is noticing that symptoms develop after a particular food. As we have said, the symptoms may be limited to the digestive system (nausea, vomiting and diarrhoea, etc.) or may include asthma, urticaria and rhinitis as well. Symptoms usually come on in a matter of minutes or a few hours at the most, and in true cases of food intolerance or allergy they always occur when that particular food is eaten. So the diagnosis can often be easy and obvious because there is such a clear-cut relation between eating a food and the onset of unpleasant symptoms. When the diagnosis is obvious there is usually no need for further tests.

However, it has been found that in people who have a violent and almost immediate reaction to fish, nuts or eggs, a skin test or RAST test will be positive in about three-quarters of cases, thus supporting a diagnosis of true allergy. But to most other foods, the skin tests are often negative. Also, to confuse matters, some people with no food allergies at all can have positive skin tests to various foods. This would indicate that a positive test does not necessarily mean that you are allergic to that food. The general message is that skin tests do not relate very well to food allergies. They may help where they agree with whatever you have noticed upsets you, but if they do not, they can simply add confusion. For example, skin tests may be negative despite violent reactions on eating a particular food either because the reaction is due to food intolerance rather than allergy, or because the skin test result is a false negative (some food extracts for skin testing must be fresh to work properly, for example). So skin tests are not much help in diagnosis, and the same applies to RAST tests.

Diagnosis of food intolerance or allergy is much more difficult when symptoms are vague and do not develop suddenly and dramatically after eating something, but are present all the time, are delayed, or come and go without any apparent relation to anything in the diet. In these cases the skin tests are usually all negative. In such cases a very careful examination of exactly what is eaten in the diet may identify the food that is causing the trouble.

Vague symptoms which are all subjective, for example headaches, generally feeling unwell, vague abdominal discomfort, depression, being unable to concentrate or sleep, are almost never due to food allergy or intolerance as far as we can tell. Although people with these often attribute them to food allergy, on further investigation they usually turn out to have major problems with their life situation, intolerable stresses and strains at home or at work, or psychological upsets like depression and anxiety. That is not to say that such symptoms are not real or that they are 'just in the mind'. The symptoms are real enough, but whenever we develop symptoms we all feel the need to attribute them to something, to a cause. Many people find that mental causes for their symptoms such as unhappiness, anguish or a major stress problem in their lives are unacceptable, as they feel that if they seek professional advice they will be written off as 'feeble-minded', 'weak-willed', 'neurotic' or 'psychiatric'. To blame symptoms on an allergy is to blame them on something external which cannot be interpreted as being your personal responsibility or fault and for which you can seek professional advice without stigma. It is almost fashionable to have an allergy, but it is not fashionable to be a neurotic or to have had a major failure with a personal relationship.

If food allergy or intolerance produce symptoms that persist for weeks or months, these are nearly always 'objective', that is, chronic diarrhoea, nausea and vomiting, asthma, recurrent attacks of urticaria, and so on.

Exclusion diets

If there is good reason to suspect a particular food or foods, then an exclusion diet may be the most reliable way of sorting it out. The suspect food is eliminated from the diet, and the symptoms vanish where the cause is allergy or intolerance. Care must be taken though. It is easy to eliminate shellfish or strawberries, but it is much more difficult to eliminate egg, cereals or dairy products because they are present in so many items of our diet.

If there are no definite suspects, yet food allergy or intolerance is thought to be present, then elimination diets can be used to try to identify the items causing trouble. However, the procedure is more complicated and time-consuming, and the results are often inconclusive. One approach is to exclude groups of foods in turn for a period of time (a week is usually sufficient) from an otherwise normal diet to see if the symptoms abate. For example, meat, fish and poultry could be excluded during the first week, then wheat, corn, and cereals the following week, then, in turn, eggs, milk, butter, and dairy products, soft fruit and citrus fruit, nuts, legumes, alcoholic drinks, tea, coffee and chocolate and so on. If the symptoms have not cleared up by one week, then allergy or intolerance is very unlikely. If elimination of a particular item leads to improvement, it can then be re-introduced to see if symptoms return. If they do, then allergy or intolerance is proven beyond reasonable doubt.

There are several other ways of doing exclusion diets. One is to start with a simple diet of items least likely to cause allergy, for example, lamb, rice, and carrots. If the symptoms get better on this diet, then items are gradually re-introduced until the culprit item is identified. It must be said, though, that if no particular food is obviously causing trouble, or if a huge list of different foods is suspected, elimination diets often give inconclusive or confusing results. Finally, these diets should be done only under supervision by an expert. Rigorous exclusion diets that continue for long periods can be hazardous to the health because they remove essential nutrients and vitamins.

Challenge tests

A challenge test relies on the patient identifying an item in the diet that may be responsible, or for an elimination diet having suggested a likely cause of the allergy or intolerance. Challenge tests can help in two ways: either to clinch the diagnosis of intolerance or allergy, or to convince someone that they do not really have an allergy or intolerance at all.

To be of any value these tests must be done under expert supervision, where neither doctor nor patient know which food is being used as a challenge; that is, the test should be 'double-blind'. Second, the food cannot be taken in the usual manner by simply eating it, as the taste and texture will give the game away (the problem may simply be one of food aversion for example). The food must be put directly into the stomach without being chewed or tasted. This can be done in two ways. In the first method, a freeze-dried sample of the food is put in a gelatine capsule, which is then swallowed whole. The capsule dissolves in the stomach to release its contents. Alternatively, a thin tube can be passed through the nose and swallowed into the stomach. The food is then made into a mixture and poured down the tube.

Challenge tests may be useful in certain rather special circumstances, but they are by no means the solution to every problem. In a recent study of children in whom food allergy was strongly suspected, about 40 per cent developed reactions in the digestive system, skin or lungs following the challenge test, but most of these children had positive skin tests to the foods involved anyway.

Unorthodox tests

As food allergy and intolerance are often blamed for a multitude of symptoms and complaints, and as true food allergy and intolerance are probably quite rare, usually resulting in clear-cut symptoms, there are many people who are convinced that they have such an allergy yet find that orthodox medicine seems to have little to offer. It is hardly surprising, then, that this is an area abounding with a variety of allergy specialists, who often charge high fees for doing tests and giving treatments for which there is little or no scientific foundation. Some of these tests we have mentioned earlier, but this is an appropriate moment to expand our previous discussion.

The pulse test was described as long ago as 1942 by Coca, one of the pioneers in allergy research. He noted that the pulse rate increased on eating a particular food causing food intolerance. Unfortunately this test has not stood the test of time and it has no value in diagnosis. Intradermal tests we have already mentioned. These are like skin-scratch or prick tests, but instead of the allergen extract being put on to the skin, and a needle being drawn through the droplet to scratch the skin, the allergen extract is actually injected into the skin with a syringe and hypodermic needle. Most experts regard intradermal tests as valueless in diagnosing food allergy. The same goes for the cytotoxic food test, where white blood cells from the allergy sufferer are exposed to various food extracts in a test tube to see if the cells die or not. Claims have been made for the sublingual food test, where drops of a dilute solution of various foods are placed under the tongue and any reaction is then noted. Apart from certain foods (in particular nuts and fish) which may cause local swelling and itching when placed under the tongue, this test has no value in diagnosis. Studies have been done showing that there was no difference between food-containing drops and 'dummy' drops.

So if my symptoms are not due to food allergy,
what are they due to?

We have already gone through the different ways in which certain chemicals in food and drink, such as caffeine or amines, can make you feel ill if you are sensitive to them.

Next, abdominal symptoms like nausea, vomiting, wind, bloating, pain, discomfort, diarrhoea and constipation can be caused by a wide range of different diseases and disorders. If you or your child have any of these persisting for more than a day or two, you must go and see your doctor. What you think is an allergy may turn out to be something else.

Finally, stress takes it out of us all in different ways. Some of us feel anxious or cannot sleep, some get headaches or chest pains, some feel generally awful, and some get abdominal symptoms. 'Food allergy' may be disguising anxiety, depression, a life crisis, a major unhappiness or even a psychiatric illness. Underlying psychological problems often come to light when endless tests for food allergy and intolerance have all proved negative in baffling cases, and these problems, once identified, can very often be sorted out successfully by correct expert counselling by appropriate health care workers.

What is the outlook for food allergy
and intolerance?

The vast majority of infants and young children grow out of their allergies as the years go by. In older children and adults, allergies and intolerance to particular foods tend to persist. Examples are allergies to fish, shellfish, nuts and some fruits. Reactions can be very severe to these, and life-long avoidance may be necessary. The outlook for people with lots of symptoms which they believe are due to food allergies is uncertain, and depends on the nature of the underlying problems causing the trouble.

Treatment of food allergy

For obvious food allergy or intolerance to a single dietary item, treatment is usually no problem. Simply avoid that item. If the allergy is to milk or eggs then avoidance is more complicated, as a wider range of foods have to be excluded from the diet. If genuine food allergy or intolerance to several commonly encountered items is present, complicated exclusion diets are very occasionally required, but these should be designed by a dietary expert so that a balanced diet is still provided and vitamin or other deficiencies do not occur. Extremes of dietary therapy are time-consuming, can be expensive, are rarely necessary and are not generally recommended. These include a total fast for five days, during which bottled spring water alone is taken, after which dietary items are gradually re-introduced. Other approaches are the 'elemental diet', where basically a special pre-digested soup of food is taken that should contain no allergens. The other types of diet we have already discussed in the section on exclusion diets. They all have their advocates but are rarely really necessary. There are several things against them. First they may not work, second they may lead to deficiencies, and third they can be extremely inconvenient to prepare and unpleasant to live with. Few children will stick to them.

If a child is obviously allergic to milk or eggs, then this should be removed from the diet. If an adult has a major reaction and becomes very ill following fish, shellfish or nuts, then these must be avoided. Otherwise, exclusion diets are probably a waste of time for most cases. Of course, there are other very good reasons for being selective about what you eat. Some people are vegetarian because they feel healthier or because they object on moral grounds to eating meat. Fresh food is generally healthier than a diet consisting entirely of processed 'junk' food. Avoidance of animal fat and a diet rich in fibre is universally acknowledged to decrease the risk of several major diseases. Dieting may be necessary if you are overweight, and a low salt diet may be recommended if you have high blood pressure. Finally, some people just feel better if they avoid certain things and if that is so, then obviously it would be stupid not to.

*Is there any medical treatment for food allergy
and intolerance?*

We discussed the anti-allergic drug sodium cromoglycate
when we talked about asthma and hayfever. This drug can also be
taken orally (Nalcrom). In theory it should prevent allergic reactions to food being triggered in the wall of the digestive system.
Trials have so far been done in infants with cow's milk intolerance,
and some of these suggest that cromoglycate may be helpful in
some cases. It has not yet been shown to be helpful in adults.
Antihistamines may help some cases of food intolerance and so
may aspirin, but discuss these with your doctor first.

Desensitization?

Sublingual desensitization – that is, putting extracts of the
offending food under the tongue – has been tried, but nobody has
ever shown it to be helpful. Other forms of desensitization are
probably useless.

Infants and food intolerance

The commonest food to cause problems in infants is cow's
milk, and it seems to be the proteins lactalbumin and lactoglobulin
to which intolerance or possibly allergy develops. Food intolerance
is much more common in infants than in older children or adults,
possibly because the digestive system of the infant is relatively
immature, so that components of the milk can either seep through
the digestive system lining and cause sensitization or produce a
direct irritant effect on the lining. Also, about one-third of
infants have low levels of the antibody called IgA, which may
be important in mopping up milk antigens before they can get
through the lining of the digestive system and cause damage. If
IgA is reduced or absent, valuable protection may be missing, but
as we said earlier there is much argument as to whether this
theory is actually correct.

In most studies, less than 1 per cent of all infants will have
cow's milk intolerance between birth and two years of age, al-

though one or two studies suggest that as many as 10 per cent may be affected. On average, symptoms begin at two months of age and they usually start between three or four weeks after the infant starts on cow's milk feeds. Cow's milk is usually the first major 'foreign' protein food encountered by an infant. As we said earlier, it remains uncertain how many reactions to cow's milk are allergic and how many are due to other mechanisms. It makes little difference from a practical point of view, so that doctors usually refer to the condition as cow's milk intolerance to avoid confusion.

What are the symptoms?

After a feed there may be an abrupt reaction almost immediately, or several hours may pass before less dramatic symptoms develop. Reactions include vomiting, diarrhoea, colic and screaming. There may be swelling of the face and lips, wheezing or development of urticaria over other parts of the body. More long drawn out and less violent symptoms include persistent diarrhoea, vague abdominal discomfort, failure to put on weight and the development of eczema. There may be changes in the mood of the infant, with irritability and fractiousness.

The diagnosis is very often obvious because of the abrupt onset of symptoms following a feed. Skin testing with milk extracts is generally not helpful. The diagnosis may be less obvious in the older child, where symptoms may be more persistent and include being generally off colour, having temper tantrums, or developing stomach ache after breakfast. It is well known that milk intolerance may start after an attack of gastro-enteritis. This may be because the infection damages the digestive system lining and allows the milk proteins to seep through, or because the infection removes the enzymes required to break down the sugars in milk.

Once a diagnosis of cow's milk intolerance has been made, cow's milk should be avoided if possible. This can have important nutritional consequences. Alternatives to cow's milk are human milk, goat's milk or soya milk, and these may act as satisfactory substitutes although intolerance can develop to them as well. Getting on to solid food is the other option. Your doctor will advise you. If for some reason cow's milk is unavoidable, then sodium cromoglycate given before feeds may help some cases. However, as we have said, this remains controversial.

Other foods that may cause intolerance in infants are eggs, fish, chicken and soya. The outlook for food intolerance in young infants is generally very good, particularly if only cow's milk is involved. It is nearly always a transient condition and clears up on its own. Most kids are free of their intolerance by their third birthday. Very occasionally an infant may have a severe reaction to a particular food. If this happens, the food should be completely avoided until the child is several years old, and then re-introduced only in a tiny amount as a test first of all.

Breast-feeding and allergy

The protective effect of breast milk in the development of allergies is controversial. The studies that have been done show variable results. Some suggest protection, some do not. Certainly two recent studies showed no decrease in the subsequent development of asthma, eczema or rhinitis in infants who were exclusively breast-fed. One theory is that babies can become sensitized to cow's milk or egg from the minute traces that are present in the mother's breast milk, that is, that the mother herself has eaten.

Coeliac disease

This condition, which is also called gluten enteropathy, is due to a reaction in the digestive system against gluten. Gluten is a protein present in wheat and other cereals. It is not yet known if the reaction to gluten in coeliac disease is allergic or not. Some evidence suggests that allergy is involved, but further research will be needed to clinch it. Whatever the true nature of the reaction to gluten, it results in considerable damage to the lining of the digestive system, and food cannot be absorbed in the normal manner. People with this condition tend to lose weight and have troublesome chronic diarrhoea. Some develop mouth ulcers and anaemia. People with coeliac disease need to take a gluten-free diet. This means that special gluten-free flour must be used for all baked products such as bread, cakes, biscuits and pastry. Flour is used in many foods such as ice cream, soups, sauces and so on, so it is quite a difficult diet to follow, but this is an example where a strict diet is very important for continued good health. Of course meat, fish, eggs, fruit and vegetables are perfectly all right.

Can other diseases of the digestive system be due to allergy?

There is much debate as to whether allergy is involved in certain forms of inflammation of the digestive system. We will discuss this in Chapter 10.

Chapter Nine

Massive Allergic Reactions.
Insect Stings and Drug Allergies

So far we have been involved with allergic reactions that take place locally in a particular organ or tissue, such as the nose or the digestive system. This usually happens when the allergen is encountered just by a single organ, for example when pollen is inhaled and sticks in the nose. What happens if a large dose of allergen is encountered by the whole body all at once? The result can be a massive allergic reaction. Such reactions usually happen when the allergen is injected directly into the blood stream, so that it quickly reaches all the tissues of the body at about the same time. Severe reactions also happen occasionally when large doses of allergen are taken by mouth rather than by injection.

Anaphylactic reactions

Massive allergic reactions are called anaphylactic reactions. Earlier this century, before antibiotics were discovered, serious infections like tetanus and diphtheria were sometimes treated by injections of horse serum. The horses from which the serum was taken had previously been injected with these germs so that the serum was rich in antibodies against them. When the antibody-rich serum was injected into someone with the infection, the antibody could combat it and so give protection (prophylaxis). Sometimes particularly if serum injections were repeated, instead of getting better a patient would have a violent and sometimes fatal reaction (anaphylaxis = without protection). This was because an allergy to the horse serum had developed. The name has stuck, so that massive allergic reactions are still called anaphylactic reactions.

Anaphylactic reactions are the most frightening, dramatic and dangerous sort of allergic reactions. They can be fatal. They usually come on very suddenly after exposure to the allergen and are often very severe, although mild reactions are also possible.

The commoner causes of anaphylactic reactions are injections of drugs to which an allergy has developed and insect stings. The other rarer causes include blood transfusion reactions, extreme allergy to foods, some sorts of anaesthetic and even severe exercise. Fortunately anaphylactic reactions are extremely rare, and even if you were a highly allergic person, you would be unlucky to get an attack. For example, it is estimated that in the USA about thirty people die each year from insect sting anaphylaxis. Anaphylactic reactions to items in food only happen to those with extreme allergies to them. The foods that can provoke anaphylactic reactions are nuts (particularly peanuts), seafood, egg albumin and some berry fruits like strawberries. We will come to the drugs and medicines that can cause anaphylaxis later in this chapter.

Basically, an anaphylactic reaction is a massive allergic reaction involving the whole body. As allergen spreads throughout the body, it triggers off a massive salvo from mast cells which fire off all together. No wonder the results can be so devastating. A few minutes after the insect sting or the injection, or eating the shellfish, there is a general feeling of fear and impending doom. The victim may even feel that he or she is going to die. This is quickly followed by a galaxy of symptoms that vary from case to case. There is flushing of the skin, and massive urticaria may develop with swelling of the face, lips, tongue and throat. The pulse races, vision becomes blurred, dizziness and faintness develop. There may be a feeling of constriction in the throat, tightening of the chest and difficulty in breathing with wheeze. The nose may become itchy and blocked and may start to run, like a sudden attack of severe hayfever. Some people develop nausea, vomiting, diarrhoea and abdominal cramp-like pains as well.

In very severe cases the blood pressure falls and the victim develops shock and loses consciousness. There may then be a period of coma followed by death. Severe anaphylactic attacks can be fatal within minutes of the injection or the sting, or attacks can be mild, without shock and unconsciousness. After the sudden acute attack, providing it is not fatal, the symptoms gradually wear off, but the urticaria can carry on for several weeks afterwards.

If you think you have had a very severe reaction to a sting, drug or food, what should you do? Obviously you must discuss it with your doctor. Skin testing can sometimes provide guidance, but this must be done and interpreted by an expert. If you have had a major reaction to a particular drug or medicine, you should consider wearing a Medic-Alert bracelet, which states what you are allergic to in case you are ever in a situation where you cannot speak for yourself. If you have had a severe reaction to a food, never eat it again. If you are eating out, avoid foods that might contain items that provoke severe reactions, or ask what is in certain dishes if you are in doubt.

The treatment for an anaphylactic reaction is an injection of adrenalin. This must be given without delay. It may be life-saving and every second counts. Bad attacks need intensive treatment in hospital. A word about the Medic-Alert Foundation. This non-profit-making organization issues bracelets or necklets briefly stating the condition you suffer from (asthma, drug allergies) in case you are ever too ill to tell the doctor yourself. It also operates a round-the-clock international telephone inquiry service for all patients on its register.

Insect stings

Basically, stinging insects deliver an injection of venom to their victims. Biting insects often inject a small amount of their saliva through the bite before sucking up their meal of blood. Allergies can develop to either. The common causes of insect allergies are stings from honey bees (who leave their stings behind in their victims), bumble bees which sting less frequently despite their large size and noisy flight, and the various members of the wasp family (not all wasps sting). Allergies can also develop to bites and stings from ants, fleas, lice, bed bugs, mosquitos and scorpions, but wasps and bees are definitely the main problem.

Bee or wasp venom is a complex mix of nasty things designed

to do harm and to damage the victim. A sting results in a painful swelling around the point of entry. Following multiple stings, the victim may feel generally unwell, with fever and headache, and may be quite ill. Sometimes an enormous swelling follows a single sting. These toxic reactions are all a direct result of the poisons in the sting and are not allergic. Sometimes the sting gets infected and becomes septic, adding further problems. Beekeepers can average about ten stings per week. Sometimes they may get heavily stung (100 or more stings), but many beekeepers who are stung regularly never get allergic reactions to the stings. On the whole, beekeepers are no more allergic than the general population.

What about allergy to bee and wasp stings? First, allergy to stings can only develop after the first sting which sensitizes a person, so that it is the second sting that leads to an allergic reaction. Because, with a sting, venom is injected directly under the skin and often reaches the blood stream quickly, the allergic reaction can be severe, and can amount to an anaphylactic reaction as we have just described. In a very allergic individual, a single sting can kill. In a non-allergic person, many stings will be unpleasant and painful, but not a major hazard to life. After a severe local reaction to a sting (a large painful lump), there is about a 5–10 per cent chance that the next sting will trigger a severe allergic reaction or even a major anaphylactic reaction. Allergies to stings are probably a bit more likely to develop in people who have other allergies as well.

Also, if insect sting allergies do develop in people with other allergies, the reactions are inclined to be more severe. Having said this, people with no other allergies at all are not exempt from becoming highly allergic to insect stings. The allergic reaction to a sting can vary from mild patches of urticaria all over the body, to anaphylaxis. Once you have had an allergic reaction to a sting, are you allergic for life? No, provided you do not get stung again for some time. Sensitization to stings does not usually last a lifetime. About 50 per cent of people lose their sensitivity as time goes by. Generally, the older you are the more severe the allergic reaction is likely to be. Children tend to get less severe allergic reactions to stings.

Diagnosis of sting allergy

This is usually obvious. A major dramatic reaction follows a few minutes after a sting. But it is often difficult to be sure (particularly with children) what sort of insect did the stinging or the biting. Skin tests and RAST tests can be useful in the diagnosis and indicate that a person is sensitized to a particular insect sting, but they must be done by an expert to be of value.

Desensitization

Insect stings are one of the few areas where no one argues about the value of desensitization injections. They work. So who should have desensitization to insect stings? If you have had an anaphylactic reaction to an insect sting, there is a 50 per cent chance that if you are stung again you will have a similar or even a worse reaction. Allergy to the sting can be confirmed by skin test, and if you have had a severe reaction then desensitization may be advisable.

How is it done?

Pure insect venom extracts are now available, and are more effective for desensitizing than extracts made from the whole insect. It is usual to give weekly injections of venom extract, starting at a very low concentration and gradually building up the strength. When a fairly high dose of venom is reached, injections are given every four to six weeks for at least two years. It may be necessary to continue for between three and five years. The injections can be stopped when the skin test or RAST test becomes negative, indicating that allergy to the venom is no longer present. Desensitization injections are effective in preventing anaphylactic reactions to further insect stings, and give 90 per cent protection. But they can themselves cause nasty reactions in about 1 per cent of cases, so they must be done by an expert.

What is the treatment of insect sting allergy?

As with so many allergic disorders, avoidance is better than cure. Avoid wasps' nests, beehives, rubbish dumps and garbage cans. On picnics and outdoor summer holidays wear insect repellent. Make sure there is always some fly-spray readily available at home in case a wasp flies in. If wasps or bees are around, cover up and wear shoes before going out.

If you or your child have had an anaphylactic reaction to an insect sting, then consult your doctor about hypo-sensitization injections. Beekeepers who are frequently stung are usually immune from severe reactions. If they are unlucky enough to develop severe allergies, the best advice is to give up beekeeping altogether and have desensitization. If they do not follow this advice they may be all right if they continue to get regular stings, but they are in danger of an anaphylactic reaction if they get heavily stung.

What to do if you get stung

Most stings result in a painful tender lump which settles in a few days. Bee stings should be gently removed, as they may go septic if left. A severe local reaction resulting in an enormous tender swelling will be soothed by a cold compress, taking some aspirin or antihistamine. For a very severe reaction, a dose of oral steroid tablets may be prescribed.

For people known to have anaphylactic reactions who are stung on the arm or leg, a tourniquet should be quickly applied to stop the venom flooding into the blood stream while they get to the nearest doctor or hospital. People who are prone to anaphylactic attacks should carry an emergency kit with them. This should contain a pre-loaded syringe of adrenalin – the antidote for anaphylaxis – so that they can give themselves a shot immediately after a sting. An alternative to injections is to munch a tablet of isoprenaline (an adrenalin-type drug) and then allow it to be absorbed into the blood stream from under the tongue. Those who get acute asthma and wheezing following stings should carry a salbutamol or adrenalin aerosol to inhale. An antihistamine tablet will help minimize some of the longer-term symptoms of anaphylaxis such as urticaria.

Drugs and anaphylaxis

There are now more drugs and medicines available to treat a huge range of conditions and diseases than ever before. The pharmaceutical industry markets hundreds of new drugs each year. Modern medicines have undoubtedly enhanced the quality of life in the latter part of the twentieth century, but there is a price to be paid, namely drug reactions. Fortunately most people do not develop them.

There are many types of reaction to drugs, most of which are probably not allergic at all. The common reactions are skin rashes, nausea, vomiting, diarrhoea, feeling ill and running a temperature. Allergic reactions to drugs are fortunately rare and range from mild to severe. First, drugs put directly on to the skin can cause allergic problems. Various creams and ointments used to treat skin conditions can occasionally cause an allergic rash, particularly if they contain antibiotics. Second, medicines and drugs taken by mouth as tablets or capsules can occasionally provoke allergic reactions, but these are uncommon and are rarely severe. Third, major allergic reactions can follow the injection of drugs and medicines. We have most knowledge about penicillin allergy, which has been closely studied over many years. Up to 2 per cent of people can develop penicillin allergy if they have repeated courses. The allergic reaction to injections varies from a mild attack of urticaria, or asthma, to a major anaphylactic reaction. Mild reactions to penicillin are far more common than severe reactions, and many are not allergic at all. It has been estimated that one person in 10,000 will have a major reaction following a penicillin injection (providing they have had penicillin before), and that 300 people die each year in the USA from major penicillin reactions. This may seem rather a lot, but when you consider the vast population of the USA, the millions of penicillin doses given each year and the lives saved as a result, then the figure is perhaps not so high. Even so, a single life lost as a result of a drug reaction is a tragedy. Skin testing is sometimes useful here, provided it is done by an expert. If you have had a penicillin reaction and your skin test to penicillin is positive, there is roughly a 50 per cent chance that you will have a reaction if you take more penicillin. If the skin test is negative, the risk is only 4 per cent or less, so skin tests can be a useful guide here. Penicillin allergy is probably over-diagnosed. Remember that antibiotics are usually taken when you are feeling ill anyway, so that reactions can be due to the illness rather than the treatment. It is reassuring that in a study of nearly 300 people who had previously had a penicillin reaction, only sixteen had a reaction when they received penicillin again. What if you really do have a penicillin allergy, and you really need to be treated with it? It is possible to desensitize penicillin-allergic people by giving them a very tiny dose to start with which will cause no upset, and then quite quickly to build the dose up to full strength.

What other drugs cause allergic problems?

Any drug or medicine that is injected can potentially lead to an allergy. The commoner ones are other antibiotics, for example sulphonamides, some anaesthetic drugs which are injected during general anaesthesia, and some local anaesthetics, for example lignocaine which is used by dentists. Blood transfusions, injections of serum, some vaccines and desensitization injections can occasionally cause trouble as well. Some tranquillizers, pain-killers and anti-inflammatory drugs like aspirin complete the list. Finally, tartrazine again (the orange azo-dye we mentioned when discussing food additives), which has been implicated as causing or aggravating asthma and hyperactivity in children. It is still used in the coloured coating of some capsules and tablets.

What is the treatment of drug allergy? If possible avoid that drug. Always tell your doctor or dentist if you have any allergies before you receive treatment or a prescription. If you are allergic to a drug that it is essential for you to take, then desensitization may be possible. Skin tests can be a helpful guide for a few drug allergies like penicillin, but not for most other drugs.

Chapter Ten

Disorders That May Have an Allergic Basis

There are a whole host of conditions that many people think are either due to allergies or at least are made worse by allergic reactions. This whole subject is a hotbed of argument and disagreement, as there is no definite evidence one way or the other. The orthodox medical view generally is that allergy has no important connection with any of these conditions, whereas some alternative healing disciplines claim that much ill health is due to 'allergy'. But by 'allergy' they usually include intolerance reactions (particularly to food) as well as the true allergic reactions we have been discussing so far in this book.

So what are these conditions and what is the evidence for their connection with allergy?

The main conditions that have been implicated are some types of migraine, some types of arthritis, hyperactivity in children and various abdominal complaints – in particular, the irritable bowel syndrome. For all these conditions there is some evidence, although it is often disputed, that allergy or intolerance – mainly to foods – may be important in some cases.

Migraine

This condition consists of severe headaches, sometimes affecting just one side of the head, often with nausea and vomiting. Sometimes vision is disturbed and flashing lights are seen. Sometimes various parts of the body become numb or weak during attacks. The cause is unknown, but it is thought to be due to changes in the blood vessels that supply the brain. It is quite a common condition, affecting women more frequently than men. As many as 10 per cent of the population will have attacks at some time. Many migraine sufferers realize that various different things can trigger attacks, such as fatigue, stress, anxiety, bright lights, long journeys, infections and premenstrual tension. Some migraine victims also find that various foods trigger off attacks. Whether this is due to a food allergy, or due to items in the diet that directly affect blood vessels in the brain (like the amine tyramine) remains undetermined. Some cases may be truly allergic, and it has been suggested that migraine is more common in people with other allergies as well.

The foods that are particularly likely to set off attacks are chocolate, monosodium glutamate (the flavour enhancer), alcohol (particularly red wine) and some cheeses. Other causes are yeast extracts, coffee, tea, vegetables such as tomatoes and beans, and fruit such as pineapple, banana and citrus fruit. Hangover headaches are due to the breakdown products of alcohol. Some people get headaches when they are very hungry and the blood glucose level is low. Some people have migraine triggered by a single type of food, others have attacks brought on by several. Studies have been done in which migraine sufferers have been put on a series of exclusion diets to see if they improve. In one such study, 82 out of 88 children had less frequent attacks of migraine when put on a simple diet consisting of just one sort of meat, one vegetable, one fruit and one sort of carbohydrate. Not all studies have been this convincing, but it is clear that for some migraine sufferers diet is important, and it often becomes obvious by a simple process of trial and error which food is triggering the attacks. Finally, there are many causes of headache. If you have persistent severe headaches go and see your doctor.

Arthritis and food intolerance

There has been enormous recent interest in the effect of diet on arthritis, and it is impossible to summarize all the work that has been done. As is so often the case with allergy, there are extreme views. Some say diet has no effect on arthritis whatsoever, others claim that a change in diet máy actually lead to a cure. And again, the truth of the matter probably lies somewhere in the middle.

First it must be said that there are many different forms of arthritis (pain, swelling and stiffness of joints) caused by many different things. Arthritis can accompany all sorts of very different diseases. For example, German measles can be complicated by a bout of arthritis, and so can many other infections. It has been known for centuries that attacks of one form of arthritis, namely gout, can be brought on by eating certain things.

Some experts now think that there is a special type of arthritis that may be due to food allergy or intolerance. Sudden attacks are usually related to eating certain things. The attacks do not last long, usually just for a few hours. They may coincide with attacks of urticaria or asthma as well, and most cases have other allergies. It tends to affect the fingers, wrists and knees, which become painful, tender and slightly swollen. There is no permanent pain, stiffness, damage or destruction of the joints involved (unlike some other types of arthritis). The foods most commonly responsible are milk and dairy products, eggs and some cereals. Skin tests are not helpful in diagnosis, which can only be based on noticing that symptoms flare up after eating certain things. The diagnosis can be confirmed by exclusion diets and challenge tests if necessary.

Rheumatoid arthritis is a common chronic and disabling form of arthritis which tends to progress with increasing deformity and destruction of the joints. No one knows the cause, but a disturbance of the immune system may be involved. Claims have been made that allergy is involved and that special diets help. Several studies have been done using these diets in patients with rheumatoid arthritis, but none have shown any benefit. It is extremely unlikely that rheumatoid arthritis is actually caused by food allergy, and whether food allergy or intolerance actually makes it worse remains to be proven. So far it does not look as if diet makes much difference, and most patients with rheumatoid arthritis who have tried special diets have been disappointed. But it must be said that there are great difficulties in doing dietary trials in arthritis. Arthritis tends to come and go of its own accord anyway, and it is also very difficult to measure accurately the symptoms of pain and stiffness.

So we must not close doors on the possibility that dietary changes might at least improve some cases of rheumatoid arthritis.

Hyperactivity in children

Hyperactive children are impulsive and excitable. They can never sit still or concentrate for any length of time. They tend to be slow learners, bad at play, unable to sit through a meal or listen to a story. They may also have disturbed sleep, and temper tantrums. Some are destructive, hostile and aggressive, but others are happy children. The hyperactive phases tend to occur in bouts lasting from a few hours to several days. Of course these features are all a bit vague and it is often difficult to decide if your child is just maddeningly boisterous, exuberant and energetic or whether the behaviour is really abnormal.

Claims have been made that hyperactivity is the result of an adverse reaction to milk or to food additives, in particular tartrazine, benzoates and nitrites. This is because bouts of hyperactivity tend to occur after eating in some cases. Studies done so far are inconclusive. Again it must be emphasized that dietary studies are very difficult to do, and the results are difficult to measure, particularly when the symptoms are rather vague. Several of the studies that have been done suggest that food additives have nothing to do with hyperactivity alone. But one study showed that dietary changes did improve some children who had both hyperactivity and migraine. So all we can say at the moment is that the issue remains open and that further studies may eventually give clearer indications as to the importance of diet in hyperactive children.

The irritable bowel syndrome

This is quite a common condition and consists of attacks of diarrhoea and abdominal pain, often alternating with periods of constipation. There may also be belching, flatulence, abdominal bloating and distention. Of course many diseases of the digestive system can produce these symptoms and your doctor will be able to diagnose these. The main point about the irritable bowel syndrome is that all the X-rays and other special tests are essentially normal. That is, there is no obvious underlying disease to account for the symptoms. Again, there is debate as to whether the cause is food allergy or intolerance. As usual, there is no clear-cut answer, but some people with irritable bowel syndrome find that attacks are triggered by various foods, and that they improve if they avoid them. Foods that are commonly associated with this condition are cereals, milk and dairy products, eggs, chocolate, coffee, tea, nuts, citrus fruit, some spices and some vegetables.

Other diseases of the digestive system

There is a group of diseases where the lining of the bowel is chronically inflamed. Ulcerative colitis is an example. There has been much debate as to whether food intolerance or allergy plays a part. Again there is no definite evidence for or against this idea, but there are reports of cases of colitis having improved when milk was excluded from the diet.

Other diseases and allergy

It has been suggested that allergy, usually to various foods, may be important in diseases such as multiple sclerosis, stomach ulcers, schizophrenia, depression, chronic ill health, neurosis, epilepsy, emotional upsets, chronic fatigue, restlessness and inability to concentrate, generalized aches and pains, 'total body allergy' and 'allergy to the twentieth century'. All that can be said is that there is no proof one way or the other, but at the moment it seems very unlikely that allergy plays any part in any of these conditions. Further careful research will be needed, but in the meantime we should perhaps keep an open mind on the subject as, if diet turns out to be important in some of these conditions after all, it raises the possibility of controlling them by means of dietary changes. Having said this, we already know that some components of the diet such as caffeine and perhaps amines like tyramine can affect mood and cause symptoms of anxiety. But apart from this, there is nothing so far from the studies that have been done to suggest that major psychological disturbances such as schizo-phrenia or depression can be caused by any particular foods.

Many people believe that they have a food allergy and that it accounts for their symptoms. These beliefs are usually incorrect. Nearly everyone has vague symptoms from time to time, and a surprisingly high number of people, perhaps as many as a third, have an aversion or dislike to a particular food. It is easy to jump to conclusions and to link the two together, but it does not follow that one is the cause of the other. Studies done on people with vague symptoms such as fatigue, depression, anxiety, headaches and abdominal discomfort which they believe to be due to food allergy have failed to show that food allergy or intolerance is re-sponsible. These people usually have underlying psychological prob-lems. True food allergy is much more likely if there are symptoms such as urticaria, rhinitis or asthma.

At the moment we must conclude that food allergy on the whole cannot be blamed for the common symptoms to which we are all prone from time to time, and the link between food allergy and psychological symptoms remains to be proven. Finally, rigorous exclusion diets may give you a psychological boost, but some are deficient in vitamins or other essential dietary components and so may actually cause ill health. Above all, if you develop symptoms that persist, go and consult your doctor about them.

PART THREE

Chapter Eleven

Alternatives to the Conventional Treatment of Allergy

Problems with the conventional treatment of allergy

Each one of us, when armed with the basic information about allergy and a bit of common sense, can probably do something to minimize our allergy if we are unlucky enough to have one. The basic rule is to identify and avoid the allergen, but this is much easier said than done, as some allergens are either very difficult to avoid because they are ubiquitous, or they may remain unidentified. Most people on developing an allergy are anxious to know what they can do for themselves, and practical tips for self-help were included and emphasized in Part 2 of this book, which dealt with the orthodox medical treatment of allergy.

Orthodox or Western medicine is largely based on a scientific approach – trying to understand how the body works in health and how it breaks down in disease. The scientific approach to the pathological processes that lead to disease has paid large dividends. There are now very many effective treatments for an enormous range of diseases, and this is why the demand for modern medicine already far exceeds supply and the economic resources to fulfil it.

Despite this major success story it is currently fashionable to criticize modern medicine on various counts. This is paradoxical, as although modern medicine is far from perfect in that it cannot cure everything, if it really had gross deficiencies presumably one would expect to find empty family practitioner surgeries and deserted hospitals. Far from it.

Many infectious diseases are now a thing of the past and only a minor health risk, thanks to inoculations and antibiotics. (However, the new virus disease AIDS poses a major challenge to science and medicine.) Many forms of cancer can be actually cured or the outlook greatly improved by modern surgery, which in turn would be impossible without modern general anaesthesia. Heart surgery, kidney transplants and dialysis machines, drugs and medicines for diabetes, high blood pressure, some types of anaemia, ulcers and asthma all save lives and enhance the quality of life by removing symptoms. The accuracy of diagnosis has also been vastly improved over the last thirty years by powerful new techniques. But one price for scientific excellence and progress in modern medicine is a 'high-tech', rather mechanistic approach to illness – and sometimes regrettably also to the people that have those illnesses.

Conventional scientific medicine has a tendency to be impersonal and detached, as it relies on identifying a particular body process that has gone wrong (say high blood pressure, which may lead to strokes and heart attacks) and then treating it so that the complications are avoided. This is the service that modern medicine gives to great effect, but sometimes at the expense of converting 'Mrs Jones with three children and financial worries' into 'the patient in bed six with high blood pressure'. Modern medicine has a mass-produced aspect to the successful delivery of effective treatment.

Coupled with this is the fact that modern medicine cannot cure everything. Some diseases are unfortunately incurable and others are very difficult to treat. Among this latter group of conditions are some of the more troublesome allergic disorders, and some of the disorders that may have an allergic basis. For these, modern medicine can still offer effective treatment in many cases, provided time and patience are employed by both patient and doctor to get the treatment right. Even so, the treatments available work by damping down or suppressing the allergic process rather than by curing it. This means that the allergy sufferer may have to take regular treatment indefinitely. If the medicines prescribed by the doctor are not entirely effective, both the doctor and the patient are likely to get increasingly frustrated and gradually the relationship between them breaks down and the patient may then be left alone to cope with symptoms. This problem is often compounded by busy doctors who do not have sufficient time to counsel allergy sufferers fully and are often accused of being unsympathetic and unwilling to take on allergy cases. It is perhaps not surprising then that allergy sufferers can become disenchanted with orthodox medicine and seek alternative forms of therapy.

Advantages of alternative or complementary medicine

Alternative medicine, meaning alternative to conventional Western medicine, is also referred to as complementary or holistic medicine. The various types of treatment included under this title are attracting increasing interest, but none of them should be accepted uncritically, very much as conventional medical treatments are constantly being subjected to scrutiny.

The potential advantages of alternative medicine are first that some cases can be helped where orthodox medicine fails. The treatments are often simple, with no complicated equipment or expensive hospitals required. Its practitioners state that alternative therapies are harmless to patients, as no powerful drugs with attendant risk of side effects are used. Alternative medicine is usually less stressful, inconvenient and unpleasant than conventional medical or surgical treatment. Both patient and therapist enter into a close one-to-one relationship, and the therapist treats the whole person rather than just a symptom, so that therapy is tailor-made to the individual requirements of the patient.

Alternative therapies are comforting, and a visit to a therapist is generally going to be a pleasant, soothing experience, which is rarely true of visits to hospitals or surgeries. The therapist usually spends much more time with you than an orthodox doctor and may be generally more sympathetic and caring. The emphasis of many alternative therapies is to treat the whole patient on many levels simultaneously, with the final aim of reaching the point where the patient can maintain good health unaided. Many therapies involve touching, which people often find soothing. Alternative therapists stress that they are not purely mechanistic in their approach, but include the spiritual needs of the whole person in an attempt to relieve suffering, or at least to teach the patient how to cope with disability by promoting self-knowledge and understanding. In fact many therapies contain an underlying vitalistic assumption regarding the patient's ability to regain health. The alternative therapist tends to be less interventionist than the conventional doctor, takes the individual as a whole and strives to bring about a return to health. The conventional doctor identifies a disease and attempts to eradicate it, but also recognizes the remarkable ability of the body to heal.

Disadvantages of alternative medicine?

Orthodox medicine largely rejects alternative therapies because there have been very few controlled trials into their effectiveness and very little research has been done. The evidence that they are effective is often anecdotal, being based on individual cases. Anecdotes are a notoriously unreliable form of evidence, as for every success story there may well be dozens of failures that we never hear about. On the other hand, many crucial discoveries in conventional medicine have been based initially on anecdotal observations which then led on to successful research. Of course it would be difficult to do controlled trials on many forms of alternative therapy because they tend to vary from patient to patient and there is often no easy end point to measure – just 'I feel better now'.

Many alternative treatments probably do not work. If something really works, the word gets around pretty quickly and everybody wants it – for example, antibiotics for serious infections or hip replacement operations for severe arthritis. On the other hand it is argued that the demand for alternative medicine is also great and is increasing. For many alternative treatments there is no theoretical scientific reason why they should work, although other sorts of explanation are offered.

A further problem resulting in part from disenchantment with orthodox medicine as regards allergy is that alternative practitioners in allergy have flourished in recent years. Some have few if any formal qualifications and little accountability over their activities. It is worth checking on qualifications and reputation before going to see them, to avoid wasting time and money.

The British Medical Association recently published a report of its three-year study into alternative medicine, which was encouraged by the Prince of Wales when he was President of the BMA in 1982. The basic conclusions of the study were that there was no proof that many of the therapies helped. Some risked harming the patient. Acupuncture, manipulation (osteopaths and chiropractors) and hypnosis were found to be helpful when done properly for certain limited conditions. Homeopathy on the other hand was said to be entirely due to a placebo effect, was found to have no rational basis, and 'worked' only in so far as both practitioner and patient believed that it did. 'Other therapies' were found to resemble primitive folk medicine and were thought to help deal with the experience of disease without actually curing it. (This in itself may be useful, as orthodox medicine often falls down here when little can be done.) Herbalism was criticized as not all the remedies are harmless. Some contain powerful and potentially toxic substances. (The BMA report has itself been heavily criticized by alternative practitioners. A main objection was that the BMA had itself not adequately examined the available evidence.)

Finally, alternative treatments for allergy contain another hazard. This is particularly true of asthma. If an alternative treatment supplants the orthodox treatment, it puts that patient at risk of having a major attack by removing effective prophylactic treatment which is the key to success in asthma.

Do alternative therapies work in allergy?

It is very difficult to give a clear answer. As we have said, there have been few trials and there is very little data to go on. Little research has so far been done, and the necessary research will be difficult to do. Alternative practitioners all have different approaches, so that comparisons between their results may not be possible. Symptoms of allergy are very variable and are difficult to measure accurately. A sensible position might be to keep an open mind, as conclusions on the value of alternative therapies would be premature in view of insufficient evidence. Some alternative therapies may be effective for some allergies, but very careful studies will be needed to show this conclusively and these will not be easy. As there is now such vast interest in both allergy and alternative medicine, there is a good chance that these difficult studies may soon be done.

How do alternative therapies work?

As we have said, some alternative treatments may help some conditions. How? By and large, the exact mechanism by which they work remains unknown. Sceptics say that if they do work it is due to their placebo (Latin: I shall be pleasing) effect. In medical terms a placebo is a medicine with no active ingredients, given to a patient to please rather than to cure. Orthodox doctors often talk about the placebo effects of various treatments. It has been repeatedly shown that if patients are given a medicine that has no active ingredient, up to 30 per cent will say they feel better, depending of course on the condition that is being treated. This obviously makes it difficult to decide if a medicine really is effective, as, in clinical studies, it has to greatly exceed 'the placebo effect' to be obviously beneficial. The argument against alternative medicine then continues by stating that any benefit derived from alternative medicine is due purely to a placebo effect. This in turn is said to be because alternative practitioners spend more time with their patients, are more compassionate and sympathetic, treat the whole person and generally function in a more 'healing' environment. Whether there is any truth in this 'anti-alternative' argument remains to be established. Recently several studies that conform to the usual medical scientific criteria indicate that acupuncture, homeopathy and hypnosis lead to improvements that cannot be explained simply by a placebo effect. Of course, the proof of the pudding is in the eating, and, if you have an allergy, and an alternative therapy works, then so much the better.

Should I go to an alternative practitioner?

If you have symptoms you should go to your family practitioner first. You may think you have an allergy, but you may be wrong. Go to the doctor for a correct diagnosis. If you have an allergy, give orthodox medicine a chance. Remember that the majority of allergy sufferers get control of their symptoms with simple effective treatment. It is true that many allergy sufferers get fed up with orthodox treatment and seek alternatives. But the reverse is also true. Many orthodox allergy specialists will tell you that time and again they see patients who have tried many alternative therapies without success and finally in frustration come to an orthodox specialist for successful diagnosis and treatment.

If you want alternative therapy, then check out the therapist's credentials or ask your own doctor to recommend a reputable practitioner, preferably one who is interested in allergy.

There are many different alternative therapies available and these include acupuncture, biofeedback, chiropractic, healing, herbal medicine, homeopathy, hypnosis, and osteopathy. The therapies to which the allergy sufferer is most likely to turn are acupuncture, homeopathy and hypnosis, so we will take a brief look at these. We will then discuss the recently established discipline of clinical ecology.

Chapter Twelve

Acupuncture, Homeopathy and Hypnosis

Acupuncture

This ancient Chinese therapy antedates modern medicine by several thousand years, and is in routine use in China for all manner of complaints. It has particular value in the relief of pain, and its efficacy in this area is no longer in doubt. Acupuncture is at the root of Chinese medical tradition, and is based on the theory that there is a connection between the internal organs and particular areas of the body surface. The whole philosophy behind acupuncture is extremely intricate and complicated, and is beyond the scope of this book. When a particular organ is diseased, stimulation or sedation of acupuncture points on the body surface can affect the 'energy' related to that organ in a beneficial way. The acupuncture points are extremely precise in their localization on the surface of the body. This stimulation is usually achieved by the insertion of fine needles, although there are other methods such as acupressure, where pressure is applied to points, or heat to specific points. This is done by the burning of herbs and is called moxibustion. Over the surface of the body there are many hundreds of acupuncture points, and these are grouped together into collections called meridians. Treatment of the various acupuncture points on the body surface within a particular meridian is said to affect the entire metabolism of the body. The skill of acupuncture is in knowing the exact location of these points, and which ones should be stimulated or sedated for any particular condition. Although symptomatic relief may be the result of acupuncture treatment, the underlying philosophy is to treat the whole body. Acupuncturists often pay great attention to subtle characteristics of the pulse at the wrist in the diagnosis of different conditions.

Most acupuncturists use fine sharp stainless steel or silver needles. The exact position of insertion is very important. The needles may be inserted and left in position for a few seconds or several minutes. Some therapists rotate the needles between finger and thumb, but exact practice varies considerably. The needles are so fine that acupuncture is usually painless. Most acupuncturists do not insert the needles to any great depth. Treatment sessions may be repeated once or twice a week until the condition is under control. Relief of symptoms may be immediate, or gradual over a matter of days after therapy, depending on the condition.

One of the main uses of acupuncture is to relieve pain. In China it is sometimes used instead of routine anaesthesia for surgical operations. It is also used for chronic conditions that can cause a lot of pain, such as arthritis and cancer. Other conditions may respond to acupuncture, such as chronic headaches, nervous problems and allergies.

Few doubt that acupuncture works in some of the situations we have described. The question is how? One theory suggests that acupuncture leads to the release within our bodies of substances called endorphins. These substances, which bear a relation to the strong pain-killing drugs morphine and heroin, have a potent pain-killing effect of their own – a sort of internal pain-control system. Another theory holds that acupuncture stimulates one set of nerves, which blocks transmission of pain impulses carried by other nerves from the diseased organ. This blocking effect is thought to happen in the spinal cord, where all the incoming nerve impulses from various parts of the body are processed and analysed before transmission to the brain. Neither theory fully explains the effects that acupuncture seems to have in conventional scientific terms. Acupuncturists have completely different theories to explain the effects. Finally, many acupuncturists both in China and in Western Europe are also medically qualifed, and those that are not often work closely with doctors.

Homeopathy

Unlike the ancient healing art of acupuncture, homeopathy in its present form is a fairly recent development and was founded by Dr Hahnemann of Leipzig in the early nineteenth century, although the original concept can be traced to antiquity. Homeopathy is based on the law of similars, that is, that 'like cures like'. Dr Hahnemann's crucial observation was that the bark of the cinchona tree, which contains quinine, the potent anti-malarial drug, if taken in large amounts by a normal person led to symptoms that resembled the disease of malaria itself. (It should be said that although the symptoms of malaria and the symptoms of quinine overdose have certain vague resemblances, there are striking differences as well.) However, Dr Hahnemann was obviously impressed and this led him on to further research, during which he found that various substances, when given to people in good health, led to symptoms that resembled various diseases. He then found that when these substances were diluted, symptoms ceased and, also, that there seemed to be a protective effect against the diseases that these noxious compounds mimicked. Surprisingly, the greater the dilution of the substance, the greater the protection that taking that substance seemed to afford. This all boiled down to the conclusion that any substance that gave symptoms similar to a disease would actually cure that same disease, if taken in tiny doses, and the more tiny the dose, the greater the effect.

Of all the alternative therapies, homeopathy in the Western world is probably the most popular. There are several homeopathic hospitals within the National Health Service in the UK, most homeopathic practitioners are also medically qualified, and many pharmacies stock homeopathic medicines. In some parts of Europe homeopathy is much more popular and is a firmly established alternative to orthodox medicine.

Homeopathists believe that the body has a wide range of self-curing mechanisms and can, if favourable circumstances permit, cope with the vast majority of illnesses unaided. Homeopathy attracts criticism from orthodox (allopathic) doctors because few controlled trials have been done and there is no obvious scientific reason why homeopathy should work in the first place. (This is not to say that there will not be an explanation, scientific or otherwise, in due course.) Orthodox practitioners usually state that where homeopathy seems to produce benefit, it is because of a placebo effect.

Even so, homeopathy is in widespread use and is a popular alternative to conventional medicine for a wide range of complaints, including allergies. Its advantages are that it is cheap and safe – because homeopathic medicines are very diluted preparations of various compounds. It is difficult to do controlled trials using homeopathic medicines because the homeopathist recognizes clusters of symptoms and prescribes accordingly. This means that therapy for each patient is individualized, which makes comparisons difficult and so makes it difficult to do the sort of studies that would prove or disprove that homeopathy really works. In fact, recent studies suggest that homeopathic medicines have a beneficial effect over and above any placebo effect, and these warrant further research.

Hypnosis

Hypnosis was popularized as a method of therapy by Anton Mesmer in the late eighteenth century. He made sweeping claims for its effectiveness in the treatment of conditions which we would now probably regard as being largely psychosomatic. With the advent of the theatre hypnotist who exploited the technique to entertain audiences, hypnosis fell into disrepute as a therapeutic method. More recently, hypnosis has been resurrected as a treatment for a limited range of conditions including some allergies, insomnia, neurotic conditions and certain forms of phobia. Hypnosis has been shown to be of some help in some cases of asthma. It can also be used to induce a state of anaesthesia for dentistry and minor operations, and people have found it useful as an aid to giving up smoking.

The hypnotist induces a particular state of consciousness in the subject. The hypnotic state is not the same as sleep, but is an altered state of mind during which the subject is amenable to accepting suggestions put to him by the hypnotist. The hypnotic state is often described as a 'hyper-suggestible' state. The suggestions can be wide-ranging, but in medicine examples of useful ones are that the arm is becoming numb so that no pain is felt or that the smell and taste of cigarettes is revolting so that the subject will never want to smoke again.

There are several ways of inducing the hypnotic state. They all rely on getting the subject to relax and concentrate on an object, perhaps the sensations coming from the left hand or some visual image. Swinging pendulums and medallions are not essential! The hypnotist talks to the subject and continues to suggest that the subject is becoming increasingly comfortable and relaxed until the hypnotic state is induced. The hypnotist then puts the desired suggestions to the subject. At the end of the session, the hypnotist quickly brings the subject out of the state. Most hypnotists who use the technique for treatment are doctors or dentists. People sometimes worry that during hypnosis they will be under the power of the hypnotist. This is not true – you cannot be made to do things against your will while in a hypnotic state. Most people can be hypnotized provided they are willing and co-operate fully with the hypnotist. Some hypnotists teach their patients to hypnotize themselves on a regular basis for treatment – auto-hypnosis. Generally hypnosis is a useful adjunct to other forms of treatment in certain conditions rather than a complete treatment in itself.

Other forms of alternative therapy

We have briefly described three popular forms of treatment that allergy sufferers may seek. There are of course dozens of other types of therapy, ranging from well-established useful healing disciplines to quackery.

Yoga, meditation, biofeedback, faith healing, herbalism and macrobiotics are just a few of the vast array of other alternatives. Maybe they work, maybe they do not. Future research should be interesting. If you must try them, it is most important that you consult your own doctor first so that an important diagnosis requiring attention is not missed and so that you do not deny yourself effective standard orthodox medical treatment for your symptoms. Unfortunately there are unscrupulous practitioners around awaiting the gullible with promises of instant cure.

Chapter Thirteen

Clinical Ecology

Food allergy and intolerance, although uncommon when compared with other allergies, undoubtedly occur, as we saw in Chapter 8, and they are most frequent in babies and young infants where milk and eggs are the main problems. The role of food allergy and intolerance in older children and adults as a cause of symptoms is uncertain and controversial. Hard facts are difficult to come by. Diet and its effect on allergies and the ability of dietary items to lead to unpleasant symptoms overlaps to an extent with the whole vast subject of diet and health generally, which we have already touched on.

The newly founded discipline of clinical ecology takes a very different view from that of orthodox medicine and holds that many substances, both in our diets and in the environment, are directly responsible for much ill health. I will try to summarize the main features of clinical ecology in this chapter.

Clinical ecology originated in the USA and was pioneered by Dr Theron Randolph – an orthodox allergist by training. His starting point was that much ill health is due to the environment we live in. Our health is affected by what we eat and drink, the contents of the air we breathe, our habits, the stresses at work and at home and the objects in our environment. Few would disagree with this. Lifestyle obviously affects health. The importance of diet and its bearing on obesity, heart attacks, high blood pressure and even cancer are becoming well known. Alcohol, tobacco and drug abuse account for much disease. Violent death on the roads due to drunken driving and suicide may relate to unhappiness and depression caused by stresses at work or at home, and exposure to poisonous chemicals in our environment obviously has adverse effects.

Where Dr Randolph departed from orthodoxy was with his concept of 'masked' or 'hidden' allergy. Actually he used 'allergy' in a very broad sense, not to mean just the classical allergic reactions due to IgE antibodies that we have been concerned with in this book, but food intolerance reactions too, and pretty well any adverse reaction to a substance or chemical in the diet or environment as well. Some of his followers do not use the term 'allergy' at all and talk about food sensitivity instead, which avoids a lot of confusion. Clinical ecologists see illness in terms of man's environment. Man is ill because of the environment. A holistic approach is adopted, that is, the whole person is considered at once even though the symptoms may be confined to one part of the body alone.

The theory continues. Much of our food is processed and packaged. It contains additives. It is high in salt content and low in vitamins when compared to fresh food. Fertilizers and weed killers contaminate the fruit and vegetables we buy. Meat may contain hormones and antibiotics given to animals to encourage their growth. The atmosphere is polluted with smoke, traffic fumes, chemicals from factories, acid rain, radioactivity and so on. Sensitivity to foods or chemicals leads to symptoms. For the clinical ecologist, typical symptoms are usually multiple, often vague and random and are not closely related to eating the offending item. Hidden or masked sensitivities develop mainly to foods that are eaten all the time in large amounts, and because we are in regular contact with the cause of the sensitivity, it is not at all obvious.

Initially there is a phase when we tolerate the food, then this tolerance breaks down and we become ill. There is an analogy with tobacco and alcohol. Initially either of these when taken make us feel ill – remember your first ever alcoholic drink or cigarette! Then we become tolerant, but eventually this tolerance breaks down and we become intolerant, and become ill as a result. In fact some clinical ecologists regard alcoholism as a form of masked allergy, rather than as an addiction. The idea seems to be that taking the food we are sensitive to initially gives us a stimulatory reaction but that this is followed by a withdrawal reaction.

Clinical ecologists recognize an evolution of symptoms throughout life. Food sensitivity usually starts early in life with colic, vomiting, diarrhoea or constipation, disturbed sleep, chronic nose problems or hyperactivity. In childhood, asthma and eczema may strike. In adult life, a vast array of symptoms may result from sensitivity, including: generally feeling ill and lethargic, inability to concentrate, insomnia, anxiety, depression, irritability and feeling tense, headaches and migraine, abdominal pain, irritable bowel syndrome and other bowel diseases, obesity, joint pains, arthritis and backache, palpitations, nasal problems, asthma, eczema, urticaria, painful periods and premenstrual tension. Obviously if dietary changes could cure this lot it would be wonderful. We will just have to wait and see if clinical ecology can deliver the goods.

How does the clinical ecologist make a diagnosis? The mainstay of diagnosis is the elimination diet. One approach is to use a five-day fast, during which only spring water is taken. By the end of the fast the symptoms should have abated. Food items are then re-introduced one by one at each meal to see if symptoms recur. This method can be a cumbersome and difficult way of reaching a diagnosis, particularly if reactions are delayed by twenty-four to forty-eight hours after eating the food, or if the symptoms are very vague.

Various other tests are used by some clinical ecologists and include intradermal skin tests and the cytotoxic test which we have discussed already. Other tests advocated by some clinical ecologists are the 'auriculo cardiac reflex test', the 'vegatest' and 'applied kinesiology'. Hair analysis is held to be useful in the diagnosis of sensitivity, the clinical ecologist identifies symptoms as stemming from sensitivity to a wide range of chemicals, including: plastics, synthetic fabrics, car exhaust fumes, deodorants, cosmetics, food additives, drugs, chemicals in tap water, cigarette smoke, paints, varnishes, polishes, cleaning agents and everyday items that contain phenol or formalin derivatives.

The basis of treatment in clinical ecology is elimination of the offending item or items from the diet, and the emphasis is on dietary manipulations to control symptoms due to sensitivities. As we have already said, if the sensitivity is to eggs, wheat or milk, avoidance may not be so easy because these items are present in so much of what we eat. Clinical ecologists claim that up to 60 per cent are helped by dietary means, and that improvement can be expected within two weeks. Lifelong avoidance may not be essential. A careful trial re-introduction can be attempted after six to nine months' abstinence. For those who cannot take exclusion diets, various forms of desensitization are advocated. Above all, if you decide to see a clinical ecologist, discuss it with your own doctor first. On no account suddenly stop any treatment that you are receiving from your own doctor without his guidance and supervision.

Chapter Fourteen

Epilogue – Allergy and the Future

If you have read this far it will be obvious to you that we are nowhere near to the last word on allergy. Perhaps we have only just started. The scientists have greatly increased our knowledge and understanding of the immunological events that lie behind allergies, but many questions remain unanswered. Why do some people get allergies and others do not? Why do some people develop that twitchiness of their bronchial tubes which leads to asthma attacks? What causes eczema and why do some people develop allergies to drugs? Is food allergy really a major health problem or will it turn out to be a blind alley?

The medical profession is becoming more sympathetic to the allergy sufferer as the problems are becoming more clearly defined. At the moment we are living in the era of modern effective pharmacology. We now have powerful drugs to treat many allergies, but there is plenty of room for improvement and newer and better anti-allergy drugs are on the horizon as research increases our knowledge. Improved understanding may also lead to more effective methods of desensitization for allergy and so to an actual cure for allergic disorders.

Alternative or complementary techniques, some of which stem from disciplines of great antiquity, have yet to prove their general utility in the treatment of allergic disease. Origin is irrelevant to value. A venerable and ancient discipline need not of necessity be efficacious. It is not just the quibbles of the orthodox medical establishment that need answering. There is the problem of common sense. If something really works for a disease, news travels fast and everyone demands it as of right. Antibiotics, appendectomies, vaccination for smallpox and polio, quinine for malaria, the drugs that cure tuberculosis, the new effective medicines for stomach ulcers and asthma, operations that cure cancer and heart disease – no form of alternative medicine has yet achieved this level of acclaim. Maybe one day one will, but I very much doubt it. The answers to allergy will probably come from scientific research. In perhaps just a few years from now we will understand the 'fine-tuning' of our immune systems so well that we will be able to intervene with subtlety – and maybe even just turn our allergies off.

USEFUL ADDRESSES

Action Against Allergy
43 The Downs
London
SW20
(Tel: 01-947-5082)

Asthma Society and Friends of the Asthma Research Council
300 Upper Street
London
N1
(Tel: 01-226-2260)

British Acupuncture Association
34 Alderney Street
London
SW1
(Tel: 01-834-1012)

British Homeopathic Association
27a Devonshire Street
London
W1
(Tel: 01-935-2163)

British Holistic Medical Association
179 Gloucester Place
London
NW1
(Tel: 01-262-5299)

Homeopathic Development Foundation Ltd
19a Cavendish Square
London
W1
(Tel: 01-629-3205)

Institute of Complementary Medicine
21 Portland Place
London
W1
(Tel: 01-636-9543)

Medic-Alert Foundation
11 Clifton Terrace
London
N4
(Tel: 01-263-8596)

National Eczema Society
Tavistock House North
Tavistock Square
London
WC1
(Tel: 01-388-4097)

FURTHER READING

Clark, T. J. H., and Godfrey, S.: *Asthma*, Chapman & Hall, London, 1983.

Knight, A.: *Asthma and hayfever*, Dunitz, London, 1981.

Lessof, M. H. (ed.): *Clinical reactions to food*, John Wiley & Sons, Chichester, 1983.

Lessof, M. H. (ed.): *Allergy, Immunological and Clinical Aspects,* John Wiley & Sons, Chichester, 1984.

Lewith, G. T., and Kenyon, J. N.: *Clinical Ecology*, Thorsons, Wellingborough, 1985.

Mann, F.: *Acupuncture – the ancient Chinese art of healing*, Heinemann, London, 1971.

Ministry of Agriculture, Fisheries and Food: *Look at the label*. Leaflet listing E numbers and what they are.

Morrow Brown, H.: *The Allergy and Asthma Reference Book*, Harper & Row, London, 1985.

Randolph, T. G., and Moss, R. W.: *Allergies: Your Hidden Enemy*, Turnstone Press, Wellingborough, 1981.

Rapp, D. J.: *Allergies and your family*, Sterling Publishing, New York, 1983.

Stanway, A.: *Alternative Medicine*, Penguin Books, London, 1982.

Stanway, A.: *Taking the Rough with the Smooth. Dietary fibre and your health*, Pan Books, London, 1981.

Index

FOR THE BEST IN PAPERBACKS, LOOK FOR THE

In every corner of the world, on every subject under the sun, Penguin represents quality and variety – the very best in publishing today.

For complete information about books available from Penguin – including Pelicans, Puffins, Peregrines and Penguin Classics – and how to order them, write to us at the appropriate address below. Please note that for copyright reasons the selection of books varies from country to country.

In the United Kingdom: For a complete list of books available from Penguin in the U.K., please write to *Dept E.P., Penguin Books Ltd, Harmondsworth, Middlesex, UB7 0DA*

In the United States: For a complete list of books available from Penguin in the U.S., please write to *Dept BA, Penguin, 299 Murray Hill Parkway, East Rutherford, New Jersey 07073*

In Canada: For a complete list of books available from Penguin in Canada, please write to *Penguin Books Canada Ltd, 2801 John Street, Markham, Ontario L3R 1B4*

In Australia: For a complete list of books available from Penguin in Australia, please write to the *Marketing Department, Penguin Books Australia Ltd, P.O. Box 257, Ringwood, Victoria 3134*

In New Zealand: For a complete list of books available from Penguin in New Zealand, please write to the *Marketing Department, Penguin Books (NZ) Ltd, Private Bag, Takapuna, Auckland 9*

In India: For a complete list of books available from Penguin, please write to *Penguin Overseas Ltd, 706 Eros Apartments, 56 Nehru Place, New Delhi, 110019*

In Holland: For a complete list of books available from Penguin in Holland, please write to *Penguin Books Nederland B.V., Postbus 195, NL–1380AD Weesp, Netherlands*

In Germany: For a complete list of books available from Penguin, please write to *Penguin Books Ltd, Friedrichstrasse 10 – 12, D–6000 Frankfurt Main 1, Federal Republic of Germany*

In Spain: For a complete list of books available from Penguin in Spain, please write to *Longman Penguin España, Calle San Nicolas 15, E–28013 Madrid, Spain*

COOKERY IN PENGUINS

Jane Grigson's Vegetable Book   Jane Grigson

The ideal guide to the cooking of everything from artichoke to yams, written with her usual charm and depth of knowledge by 'the most engaging food writer to emerge during the last few years' – *The Times*

More Easy Cooking for One or Two   Louise Davies

This charming book, full of ideas and easy recipes, offers even the novice cook good wholesome food with the minimum of effort.

The Cuisine of the Rose   Mireille Johnston

Classic French cooking from Burgundy and Lyonnais, including the most succulent dishes of meat and fish bathed in pungent sauces of wine and herbs.

Good Food from Your Freezer   Helge Rubinstein and Sheila Bush

Using a freezer saves endless time and trouble and cuts your food bills dramatically; this book will enable you to cook just as well – perhaps even better – with a freezer as without.

An Invitation to Indian Cooking   Madhur Jaffrey

A witty, practical and delightful handbook of Indian cookery by the much loved presenter of the successful television series.

Budget Gourmet   Geraldene Holt

Plan carefully, shop wisely and cook well to produce first-rate food at minimal expense. It's as easy as pie!

FOR THE BEST IN PAPERBACKS, LOOK FOR THE 🐧

COOKERY IN PENGUINS

Mediterranean Food   Elizabeth David

Based on a collection of recipes made when the author lived in France, Italy, the Greek Islands and Egypt, this was the first book by Britain's greatest cookery writer.

The Complete Barbecue Book   James Marks

Mouth-watering recipes and advice on all aspects of barbecuing make this an ideal and inspired guide to *al fresco* entertainment.

A Book of Latin American Cooking   Elisabeth Lambert Ortiz

Anyone who thinks Latin American food offers nothing but *tacos* and *tortillas* will enjoy the subtle marriages of texture and flavour celebrated in this marvellous guide to one of the world's most colourful *cuisines*.

Quick Cook   Beryl Downing

For victims of the twentieth century, this book provides some astonishing gourmet meals – all cooked in under thirty minutes.

Josceline Dimbleby's Book of Puddings, Desserts and Savouries

'Full of the most delicious and novel ideas for every type of pudding' – *Lady*

Chinese Food   Kenneth Lo

A popular step-by-step guide to the whole range of delights offered by Chinese cookery and the fascinating philosophy behind it.

A New Book of Middle Eastern Food   Claudia Roden

'It has permanent value' – Paul Levy in the *Literary Review*. 'Beautifully written, interesting and evocative' – Josceline Dimbleby in the *Sunday Telegraph*. This revised and updated edition of *A Book of Middle Eastern Food* contains many new recipes and much more lore and anecdote of the region.

The Pleasure of Vegetables   Elizabeth Ayrton

'Every dish in this beautifully written book seems possible to make and gorgeous to eat' – *Good Housekeeping*

French Provincial Cooking   Elizabeth David

'One could cook for a lifetime on this book alone' – *Observer*

Jane Grigson's Fruit Book

Fruit is colourful, refreshing and life-enhancing; this book shows how it can also be absolutely delicious in meringues or compotes, soups or pies.

A Taste of American Food   Clare Walker

Far from being just a junk food culture, American cuisine is the most diverse in the world. Swedish, Jewish, Creole and countless other kinds of food have been adapted to the new environment; this book gives some of the most delicious recipes.

Leaves from Our Tuscan Kitchen   Janet Ross and Michael Waterfield

A revised and updated version of a great cookery classic, this splendid book contains some of the most unusual and tasty vegetable recipes in the world.

The Best of Eliza Acton   Selected and Edited by Elizabeth Ray
With an Introduction by Elizabeth David

First published in 1845, Eliza Acton's *Modern Cookery for Private Families*, of which this is a selection, is a true classic which everyone interested in cookery will treasure.

Easy to Entertain   Patricia Lousada

Easy to Entertain hands you the magic key to entertaining without days of panic or last minute butterflies. The magic lies in cooking each course ahead, so that you can enjoy yourself along with your guests.

French Provincial Cooking   Elizabeth David

'It is difficult to think of any home that can do without Elizabeth David's *French Provincial Cooking* . . . One could cook for a lifetime on the book alone' – *Observer*

The National Trust Book of Traditional Puddings   Sara Paston-Williams

'My favourite cookbook of the year. Engagingly written . . . this manages to be both scholarly and practical, elegant without pretension' – *Sunday Times*

The New Book of Middle Eastern Food   Claudia Roden

'This is one of those rare cookery books that is a work of cultural anthropology and Mrs Roden's standards of scholarship are so high as to ensure that it has permanent value' – Paul Levy in the *Observer*

The Adventurous Gardener   Christopher Lloyd

Prejudiced, delightful and always stimulating, Christopher Lloyd's book is essential reading for everyone who loves gardening. 'Get it and enjoy it' – *Financial Times*

The Magic Garden   Shirley Conran

The gardening book for the absolute beginner. 'Whether you have a window box, a patio, an acre or a cabbage patch . . . you will enjoy this' – *Daily Express*

The Cottage Garden   Anne Scott-James

'Her history is neatly and simply laid out; well-stocked with attractive illustrations' – *The Times*. 'The garden book I have most enjoyed reading in the last few years' – *Observer*

Growing Fruit   Mary Spiller

From blossom to harvest, through planting, pruning, picking and storing, in a small or large garden, plot or pot, here is an illustrated step-by-step guide to growing fruit of all kinds.

The Illustrated Garden Planter   Diana Saville

How to choose plants for your garden – to cover a wall, creep between paving, provide colour in summer – and to plan for collective effect or to overcome a difficult site. 650 plants are illustrated, in all over 900 described.

Organic Gardening   Lawrence D. Hills

The classic manual on growing fruit and vegetables without using artificial or harmful fertilizers. 'Enormous value . . . enthusiastic writing and off-beat tips' – *Daily Mail*

GARDENING IN PENGUINS

The Penguin Book of Basic Gardening Alan Gemmell

From the perfect lawn to the flourishing vegetable patch: what to grow, when to grow and how to grow it. Given the garden, a beginner can begin on the day he buys this book with its all-the-year-round Gardener's Calendar.

The Pip Book Keith Mossman

All you need is a pip and patience . . . 'The perfect present for the young enthusiast, *The Pip Book* should ensure that even the most reluctant avocado puts down roots and sends up shoots' – *The Times*

The Town Gardener's Companion Felicity Bryan

The definitive book for gardeners restricted by the dimensions of their gardens but unrestrained by their enthusiasm. 'A fertile source of ideas for turning a cat-ridden concrete backyard into a jungle of soothing green' – *Sunday Times*

Water Gardening Philip Swindells

A comprehensive guide to the pleasures and uses of expanses of water, however great or small in the garden. Includes advice on aquatic and marginal plants and the management of ornamental fish.

Beat Garden Pests and Diseases Stefan Buczacki

An invaluable book, covering all types of plants, from seedlings to root vegetables . . . there is even a section on the special problems of green-houses.

The Englishman's Garden Alvide Lees-Milne and Rosemary Verey

An entrancing guided tour through thirty-two of the most beautiful individual gardens in England. Each garden is lovingly described by its owner. Lavishly illustrated.

Audrey Eyton's F-Plus   Audrey Eyton

'Your short-cut to the most sensational diet of the century' – *Daily Express*

Caring Well for an Older Person   Muir Gray and Heather McKenzie

Wide-ranging and practical, with a list of useful addresses and contacts, this book will prove invaluable for anyone professionally concerned with the elderly or with an elderly relative to care for.

Baby and Child   Penelope Leach

A beautifully illustrated and comprehensive handbook on the first five years of life. 'It stands head and shoulders above anything else available at the moment' – Mary Kenny in the *Spectator*

Woman's Experience of Sex   Sheila Kitzinger

Fully illustrated with photographs and line drawings, this book explores the riches of women's sexuality at every stage of life. 'A book which any mother could confidently pass on to her daughter – and her partner too' – *Sunday Times*

Food Additives   Erik Millstone

Eat, drink and be worried? Erik Millstone's hard-hitting book contains powerful evidence about the massive risks being taken with the health of consumers. It takes the lid off the food we eat and takes the lid off the food industry.

Pregnancy and Diet   Rachel Holme

It *is* possible to eat well and healthily when pregnant while avoiding excessive calories; this book, with suggested foods, a sample diet-plan of menus and advice on nutrition, shows how.

PENGUIN HEALTH

Medicines: A Guide for Everybody   Peter Parish

This fifth edition of a comprehensive survey of all the medicines available over the counter or on prescription offers clear guidance for the ordinary reader as well as invaluable information for those involved in health care.

Pregnancy and Childbirth   Sheila Kitzinger

A complete and up-to-date guide to physical and emotional preparation for pregnancy – a must for all prospective parents.

The Penguin Encyclopaedia of Nutrition   John Yudkin

This book cuts through all the myths about food and diets to present the real facts clearly and simply. 'Everyone should buy one' – *Nutrition News and Notes*

The Parents' A to Z   Penelope Leach

For anyone with a child of 6 months, 6 years or 16 years, this guide to all the little problems involved in their health, growth and happiness will prove reassuring and helpful.

Jane Fonda's Workout Book

Help yourself to better looks, superb fitness and a whole new approach to health and beauty with this world-famous and fully illustrated programme of diet and exercise advice.

Alternative Medicine   Andrew Stanway

Dr Stanway provides an objective and practical guide to thirty-two alternative forms of therapy – from Acupuncture and the Alexander Technique to Macrobiotics and Yoga.

PENGUIN HEALTH

A Complete Guide to Therapy   Joel Kovel

The options open to anyone seeking psychiatric help are both numerous and confusing. Dr Kovel cuts through the many myths and misunderstandings surrounding today's therapy and explores the pros and cons of various types of therapies.

Pregnancy   Dr Jonathan Scher and Carol Dix

Containing the most up-to-date information on pregnancy – the effects of stress, sexual intercourse, drugs, diet, late maternity and genetic disorders – this book is an invaluable and reassuring guide for prospective parents.

Yoga   Ernest Wood

'It has been asked whether in yoga there is something for everybody. The answer is "yes"'   Ernest Wood.

Depression   Ross Mitchell

Depression is one of the most common contemporary problems. But what exactly do we mean by the term? In this invaluable book Ross Mitchell looks at depression as a mood, as an experience, as an attitude to life and as an illness.

Vogue Natural Health and Beauty   Bronwen Meredith

Health foods, yoga, spas, recipes, natural remedies and beauty preparations are all included in this superb, fully illustrated guide and companion to the bestselling *Vogue Body and Beauty Book*.

Care of the Dying   Richard Lamerton

It is never true that 'nothing more can be done' for the dying. This book shows us how to face death without pain, with humanity, with dignity and in peace.